PSYCHOLOGY OF EMOTIONS, MOTIVATIONS AND ACTIONS

SUICIDAL IDEATION

PREDICTORS, PREVALENCE AND PREVENTION

PSYCHOLOGY OF EMOTIONS, MOTIVATIONS AND ACTIONS

Additional books in this series can be found on Nova's website under the Series tab.

Additional e-books in this series can be found on Nova's website under the e-book tab.

PSYCHOLOGY OF EMOTIONS, MOTIVATIONS AND ACTIONS

SUICIDAL IDEATION

PREDICTORS, PREVALENCE AND PREVENTION

BRADLEY WEAVER
EDITOR

nova publishers
New York

Library of Congress Cataloging-in-Publication Data

Suicidal ideation : predictors, prevalence and prevention / editor, Bradley Weaver.
pages cm. -- (Psychology of emotions, motivations and actions)
Includes index.
ISBN 978-1-63483-092-8 (hardcover)
1. Suicidal behavior. 2. Suicide--Prevention. I. Weaver, Bradley.
RC569.S8955 2015
616.85'8445--dc23

2015019817

Published by Nova Science Publishers, Inc. † New York

CONTENTS

PREFACE

Suicidal ideation may be defined as any self-reported thoughts of engaging in suicide related behavior. The first chapter provides a comprehensive definition of the concept of suicidal ideation together with related epidemiological data and then reviews the major risk factors. The possible controversial role of early experiences of childhood abuse and neglect in the development of suicidal ideation are explored. The impact of universal, selective and indicated suicide prevention strategies in lowering suicide rates are analyzed as well. The authors of the remaining chapters of the book review the suicidal symptoms among veterans with Chronic PTSD; recent advances in antidepressant drugs research; hypotheses for the pathogens of the rarely occurring antimicrobial-induced mania and suicide; and suicide prevention methods using the internet.

Chapter 1 - Suicidal ideation may be defined as any self-reported thoughts of engaging in suicide- related behavior. It is commonly considered the first step of the suicide process, beforesuicidal planning and suicidal act, the outcome of which may be fatal or not. Its lifetime prevalence ranges from 2.6% to 25.4% in the general population according to different countries, sex, and age groups and its relationship with suicidal planning ranges from 5% to 96%. This review chapter first aimed to provide a comprehensive definition of the concept of suicidal ideation together with providing related epidemiological data and then to review the major risk factors for suicide such as the positive history of previous suicide attempts, the association with psychiatric and physical conditions, low social support, and stressful life events. The authors also aimed to investigate the paths leading from ideation to suicidal acts providing some useful tools for the identification and evaluation of suicidal ideation in the clinical practice. Furthermore, the possible controversial role of early childhood experiences, abuse and neglect in the development of suicidal ideation will be explored. Finally, the impact of universal, selective, and indicated suicide prevention strategies in lowering suicide rates will be analyzed.

Chapter 2 - Since 2001, more than 2.2 million American Veterans have served in Afghanistan (Operation Enduring Freedom, or OEF) and in Iraq (Operation Iraqi Freedom, or OIF). PTSD is the most frequently diagnosed mental disorder among OIF/OEF Veterans seeking care through the Department of Veterans Affairs, and the current prevalence of PTSD among military veterans is estimated at 8%. The prevalence rate for suicide in the US military has increased substantially since 2005. Data from the National Comorbidity Study (NCS) demonstrated that PTSD is independently associated with suicide attempts in the general population (adjusted odds ratio = 1.81; 95% CI: 1.45-2.26). PTSD has also been shown to predict completed suicides among military veterans. Recent studies have demonstrated that PTSD is a significant risk factor for suicidal ideation in Iraq and Afghanistan War Veterans, and for suicide attempts and for completed suicide in the general population. PTSD has been shown to be associated with an increased risk of suicidal ideation even among PTSD diagnosed persons who are not dually diagnosed with either MDD or AUD. Thus, PTSD and PTSD-related suicidality are pressing current public health concerns among veterans and non-veterans.

The long term course of PTSD and PTSD-related suicidality is less well characterized than the acute course of those conditions. Survival analysis data from the NCS study demonstrated that more than one third of people with an index episode of PTSD fail to recover even after many years, so the authors of that paper concluded that PTSD is often persistent. Similarly, a review of the literature by Santiago and colleagues (2013) concluded that 39% of those with PTSD have a chronic course. Spiro et al. (1994) reported that those exposed to moderate or heavy combat in WWII had 13 times greater risk of PTSD decades later. In a review of the literature, Falk and colleagues (1994) reported that older adults meet diagnostic criteria for PTSD as many as 45 years after trauma. Similarly, Dirkzwager et al. (2001) found PTSD symptoms to be present four decades after exposure to combat among older Dutch veterans of World War II. A significant association has also been reported among veterans aged 65 and older between PTSD and suicidal ideation. PTSD among older adults in the United States is associated with considerable psychiatric comorbidity and psychosocial dysfunction, and with mood and anxiety disorders. The association of PTSD and suicidality is not well studied in the elderly. By 2010, nearly 40% of American veterans were at least 65 years old, emphasizing the need to understand the impact of PTSD and other negative effects of military service on the mental and physical health of aging veterans. Thus, chronic PTSD and PTSD-related suicidality are pressing current public health concerns among older veterans and non-veterans.

The DSM-5 diagnostic system was officially approved in 2013. The DSM-5 system for PTSD lists 20 possible symptoms and signs, grouped into four (rather than the previous three) clusters, including intrusion symptoms, avoidance, hyper-arousal, and affective symptoms (negative alterations in cognitions and mood associated with the traumatic events) (APA, 2013). The new diagnostic cluster in the proposed diagnostic system for PTSD, which was not present in DSM-IV, involves negative alteration in cognitions and mood associated with the traumatic event, as evidenced by two or more of seven listed symptoms. Thus, the diagnostic criteria for PTSD in DSM-5 have been broadened to include some depressive symptoms, (Criterion C). For the first time, some depressive symptoms (which could be associated with suicidal ideations) are now part of the diagnostic criteria for PTSD in the DSM-5, though the presence of suicidal ideations is not specifically mentioned in the DSM-5 criteria for PTSD. In contrast, diagnostic criteria for PTSD in the DSM-IV did not include any mention of depressive symptoms, but instead included only symptoms associated with anxiety. Other smaller changes were also included in the DSM-5 diagnostic criteria for PTSD, though a discussion of those smaller changes is beyond the scope of this manuscript. Field trials were recently conducted to assess the reliability of selected categorical DSM-5 diagnoses, including PTSD, as obtained by two independent clinicians. That published manuscript reported "very good" diagnostic reliability for the DSM-5 diagnosis of PTSD in the recently conducted DSM-5 field trials. Specifically, that field trial reported a Kappa value of 0.67 for PTSD, which was higher than that for such well-established diagnoses as major depressive disorder, bipolar disorder, alcohol use disorder, and borderline personality disorder. Thus, there is recent empirical evidence from field trials which provides preliminary support for the reliability of the new diagnostic criteria for PTSD in the DSM-5, including the inclusion of depressive symptoms as one of the diagnostic criteria for PTSD. However, it is unclear whether findings concerning PTSD in younger veterans apply to chronic PTSD noted in elderly veterans (Averill & Beck, 2000). Also, the prevalence of suicidal symptoms and other depressive symptoms in veterans with PTSD, including chronic PTSD, remains unclear.

The study described in the current report sought to characterize the clinical picture of chronic PTSD among veterans presenting for treatment at a Veterans Affairs facility, and to assess the prevalence of suicidal ideation and suicidal behavior among those veterans. It was hypothesized that chronic PTSD noted in that sample of veterans would be characterized by prominent depressive symptoms, including prominent suicidal symptoms.

Chapter 3 - Despite widely clinical applications, during the early 1990s, emergence the episodes of patients' suicide receiving antidepressants, especially in children was reported. As for 2004, the US and European regulatory authority began implementing verification programs to assess the influence on suicidal behavior from the use of antidepressants. With the increasing number of cases reported, several newly developed antidepressants are facing withdrawn from the market. Although the underlying mechanisms of action for drugs-induced suicide remained unclear, researches focusing on revealing the relationship between efficacy and toxicities of antidepressants have been initiated in China and US. To counteract this situation, genetic study of anti-depressant induced suicidal behaviors and other toxicity episode has been started. More than one hundred research papers, perspectives and reviews have been published. This chapter will depict the recent advances of these researches and offers the possible initiations for future investigations.

Chapter 4 - In 2002, Abouesh's reviewed the phenomenon of rarely occurrences of spontaneous antimicrobial-induced mania in western world. Lately, increasing cases and reports of clinical evidence have supported this issue again and again, especially in kids and teenagers. Yet the mechanisms of action for the relationship of this phenomenon behind the scenario are still missing. After carefully analyzing references and reports, the authors have found that it is very similar with their previous suggests the relationship between patient suicide by antidepressant treatments and human genetic factors. Thus the authors speculate the some drug-induced toxicological characters vs the therapeutic efficacies and mechanisms of action of different types of drugs by genetics and bioinformatics considerations and investigations. Further explanations from many newly published data and references are enlisted and separately analyzed. Comparisons and mechanistic investigation borrowed from the work of other categories of drugs and neural toxicity types are also highlighted in this chapter.

Chapter 5 - In communities including many people with high suicide risk nurturing gatekeepers are effective in preventing suicide. Evidence regarding suicide prevention through gatekeeping has been obtained at a quasi-experimental level. In recent years, novel attempts have been made to provide a basis for gatekeeping, such as extracting internet data indicating a high risk of suicide. Associations between suicide rates and web searches or Twitter use including suicide-related keywords have been reported in a large number of studies. These studies suggest the possibility of guiding people with high risk of suicide toward help resources by placing advertisements on the web. In Japan, a private non-profit organization called OVA has been engaged in online gatekeeping since 2013, by using search advertising techniques for those at high risk of suicide.

This chapter describes the online gatekeeping practice and discusses the feasibility and effects of online gatekeeping. Given the growing rate of Internet use worldwide, the authors should consider the effective utilization of this technology in order to prevent suicide.

In: Suicidal Ideation
Editor: Bradley Weaver
ISBN: 978-1-63483-092-8

Chapter 1

SUICIDAL IDEATION: A COMPREHENSIVE OVERVIEW

Gianluca Serafini*, Paola Solano* and Mario Amore
Department of Neuroscience, Rehabilitation, Ophthalmology, Genetics, Maternal and Child Health (DINOGMI), Section of Psychiatry, University of Genoa, Genoa, Italy

ABSTRACT

Suicidal ideation may be defined as any self-reported thoughts of engaging in suicide- related behavior. It is commonly considered the first step of the suicide process, before suicidal planning and suicidal act, the outcome of which may be fatal or not. Its lifetime prevalence ranges from 2.6% to 25.4% in the general population according to different countries, sex, and age groups and its relationship with suicidal planning ranges from 5% to 96%. This review chapter first aimed to provide a comprehensive definition of the concept of suicidal ideation together with providing related epidemiological data and then to review the major risk factors for suicide such as the positive history of previous suicide attempts, the association with psychiatric and physical conditions, low social support, and stressful life events. We also aimed to investigate the

* Correspondence: Gianluca Serafini M.D., Ph.D. and Paola Solano M.D., Department of Neuroscience, Rehabilitation, Ophthalmology, Genetics, Maternal and Child Health (DINOGMI), Section of Psychiatry, University of Genoa, IRCCS San Martino, Largo Rosanna Benzi 10, 16100, Genoa, Italy; e.mail: gianluca.serafini@unige.it; paola.solano@alice.it.

paths leading from ideation to suicidal acts providing some useful tools for the identification and evaluation of suicidal ideation in the clinical practice. Furthermore, the possible controversial role of early childhood experiences, abuse and neglect in the development of suicidal ideation will be explored. Finally, the impact of universal, selective, and indicated suicide prevention strategies in lowering suicide rates will be analyzed.

Keywords: Suicidal ideation, suicide risk, suicide prevention, suicide predictors

INTRODUCTION

Suicide is the fourteen cause of death in the world and, overall, it represents 1.5% of all deaths. The World Health Association (WHO) estimates that in 2020 the number of suicides will reach approximatively million and half per year, i.e. one suicide every 40 seconds (Wyder & DeLeo, 2007). Data suggested that at least 5-10% (Kessler et al., 1999; Weissman et al., 1999;Hawton &Van Heeringen, 2009) of the general population has attempted suicide once in life.

The positive history of suicide attempts is one of the major risk factor for completed suicide (Hawton & Van Heeringen, 2009) recurring in approximately 40% of suicide victims (Cavangh et al., 2003). Furthermore, the existing literature shows that repeated suicide attempts considerably increase suicide risk (Rudd, 2006) and that one fifth of those who attempt suicide will repeat this behavior within one year from the former. Notably, of these repeaters 1 to 6% will die by suicide (Christiansen & Jensen, 2007; Scoliers et al., 2009; Nordstrom et al., 1995; Owens et al., 2002).

Suicidology, the discipline that concerned the study of suicidal behaviors, thoroughly investigates the "suicide process" trying to identify the fundamental steps leading subjects to attempt as well as to complete suicide.

This chapter is mainly focused on the concept of suicidal ideation that has been recognized as the first critical step within the suicidal process in order to provide a comprehensive background that could foster the development of effective prevention strategies together with guiding clinicians in the early recognition of suicidal risk.

Definition

Suicidal behavior might be described as a variable process of that usually stretches over many years and ranges from suicidal ideation that is defined as thoughts about the worthlessness of life and death wishes, to concrete planning finally ending in suicide attempts (Wyder & DeLeo, 2007; Hawton &Van Heeringen, 2009). The study of such process in the general population is important for the prediction of potentially preventable /(or avoidable?) deaths, and the relief and monitoring of the high level of distress due to this behavior. However, there is not an univocal terminology in the current literature for suicidal behaviors and the inclusion of suicidal ideation throughout the suicide process is still a complex and controversial issue (WHO, 2014).

Once, literature claimed that suicide completers and attempters were different populations with different intents (Stengel, 1964), though this conceptualization failed to include those suicide attempts that did not end out in completed suicides by chance. Therefore, the term "parasuicide" has been suggested to address those behaviors that were carried out with no lethal intent (Kreitman, 1969).

Edwin Shneidman, in "Definition of suicide" (Shneidman, 1985), further explores the difficulties in choosing a shared terminology to address suicidal behaviors. Shneidman (1985) underlines the relationship between suicide attempts and completed suicides, which, in his opinion, would differ only for the outcome, namely lethal or not lethal. Therefore, the definition "suicide attempt" should be reserved to those "completed suicides that fortuitously survived" (Shneidman, 1985, p.19). In the absence of lethal intent, Shneidman (1985) suggests the use of the term "parasuicide". Similarly to Shneidman (1985), O'Carroll and colleagues (1996) in their conceptualization (aiming to systematize the terminology of suicidal behaviors) suggested to use the term "suicide attempts" for those behaviors that were carried out with lethal intent and dismissing the term "parasuicide" due to its excessive broadness. Sheidman (1993) further suggested the term "suicidality" to designate an individual's risk level of danger to himself, though some other authors refer to suicidal ideation when using this term (Bertolote & Wasserman, 2009).

The WHO Multicentre Study on Parasuicide suggested the interchangeability of the terms "parasuicide" and "suicide attempts" (De Leo et al., 2006) and defines "suicide attempt" as "an act with nonfatal outcome, in which the individual deliberately initiates a non- habitual behavior that, without intervention from others, will cause self-harm, or deliberately ingests a substance in excess of the prescribed or generally recognized therapeutic dosage, and which is aimed at realizing changes which the subject desired via the actual or expected physical consequences" (Bille-Brahe et al., 1994, p.7; Schmidtke et al., p.8). Unfortunately, this descriptive definition does not consider the subject's intention nor the severity of the act (Bertolote & Wasserman, 2009). Silverman and colleagues (2007a, 2007b) argued that the intention beyond suicidal behaviors is of paramount importance for its definition and understanding. These authors suggested that a suicide attempt is "a self-inflicted and potentially injurious behaviors with no fatal outcome for which there is a clear – explicit or implicit - evidence of intent to die" (Silverman et al., 2007b, p.273). There is agreement in defining suicidal ideation as "any self-reported thoughts of engaging in suicide related behavior" (Bertolote & Wasserman, 2009). Moreover, a recent study evaluating the interrater reliability of Silverman and colleagues' nomenclature for suicidal ideation, behavior and communication on 198 case records showed a moderate reliability for suicidal ideation (kappa value 0,476) and suicidal behavior (kappa value 0,502), whereas a low reliability for suicidal communication (kappa value 0,016) has been reported (Kattimani et al., 2015). These results were confirmed when the stated intent item of the Pierce Suicide Intent Scale (PSIS) was correlated with suicidal ideation and behavior as assessed using the Silverman et al. nomenclature (Kendall tau 0.723 and 0.747, respectively). However, the relationship between suicide-related communication and the mentioned intent item on the PSIS resulted weak albeit statistically significant (Kattimani et al., 2015).

Suicidal Process

Suicide occurs at the end of a process that was originally described by Zubin (1974) who suggested that it should be considered as a result, an outcome. This concept has later been further investigated and several models have been developed such as the "stress-diathesis model" (Mann et al., 2010) as well as the "stress – vulnerability model" (Wasserman, 2001). Furthermore, the concept of "scarring" (Post, 1992), i.e. vulnerability accumulation, has been applied to suicidal behaviors by Van Heeringen and colleagues (2000) who showed that once a subject has entered it (i.e. experienced suicidality), he or she may become more vulnerable to future suicidal behavior as a result. According to this model, later stages of the suicidal process are more autonomous than the earlier ones often triggered by external events and hence perhaps, less amenable to prevention.

In summary, all these models have in common a sequence that goes from suicidal ideation through death wishes, suicide contemplation, suicidal planning to suicidal act whose outcome can be fatal or not (Zubin, 1974). However, this does not mean that every suicidal ideation will end up in a suicidal act. The above mentioned sequence reflects a clinical perspective and tried to reconstruct the process backwards from a suicide attempt.

EPIDEMIOLOGY

The epidemiological study of suicidal ideation should carefully consider the existence of cultural differences among countries that may, no doubt, influence its–conceptualization, the meaning and manner through which the suicidal process develops. This has been highlighted by the WHO- Multisite Intervention Study on Suicidal Behaviors (SUPRE-MISS) that explored the relationship between suicidal ideation and other components of the suicidal spectrum. The community survey component of SUPRE-MISS (Bertolote et al., 2005) consisted of interviews which were conducted with subjects within the general populations of nine cities: Brisbane (Australia); Campinas (Brazil); Chennai (India); Colombo (Sri Lanka); Durban (South Africa); Hanoi (Vietnam); Karaj (Iran); Tallin (Estonia); Yuncheng (China).

Overall, approximately 20000 subjects were interviewed by nurses, psychologists, medical students, doctors and public health professionals, previously trained to use the survey instrument. These instruments had been employed by the European Parasuicide Interview Schedule (Kerkhof et al., 1999) and applied in the WHO/EURO multicentre study on suicidal behaviors. The key questions for assessing suicidal ideation, planning, and attempts were as follows:

1. Have you ever seriously thought of committing suicide?
2. Have you ever made a plan for committing suicide?
3. Have you ever attempted suicide?

In the case of positive response, further questions concerning the age and how long ago' suicide thoughts, plans or attempts occurred were more deeply investigated according to the protocol.

The proportion of subjects who reported lifetime suicidal ideation varied from 25,4% (Durban) to 2,6% (Chennai). Those having planned a suicidal act varied from 15,2% (Durban) to 1,1% (Hanoi) and the proportion of suicide attempts ranged from 4,2% (Brisbane and Karaj) to 0,4% (Hanoi). The factor variation for suicidal ideation was 9,8 (i.e. in Durban subjects were 9,8 times more likely to report suicidal ideation when compared to Chennai individuals). Concerning other additional variables, the factor variation was 13,8 for suicidal planning and 10,5 for suicide attempts (Bertolote et al., 2010). A common feature for all sites was the decreasing gradient between ideation and planning as well as between planning and attempts. However, there were differences among the way of decreasing as well as the relationship between the components of the suicidal process in the different sites. For instance, in Brisbane 96% of those who reported suicidal ideation also planned suicide and 38% of them attempted suicide, whereas in Hanoi 13% of suicidal ideators planned the act and only 5% attempted suicide (Bertolote et al., 2005). Moreover, comparing suicidal ideation to suicidal planning in the SUPRE-MISS sites, a significant discrepancy between their proportion ranging from 96% in Brisbane to 5% in Hanoi appeared. These data suggested the existence of differences in moving from suicidal thoughts to plans in different cultures. Considering the comparison between suicidal ideation and suicide attempts, their proportion ranged from 62% in Chennai to 5% in Hanoi (i.e. the majority of subjects who attempted suicide in Chennai reported to have passed through suicidal ideation, while this occurred only in the 5% of the interviewed subjects in Hanoi) (Bertolote et al., 2010).

The importance of suicidal ideation in relationship with the severity of suicide attempts was evaluated in the SUPRE-MISS. The results ranged from a virtual lack of relationship between these variables to a symmetrical and inverted association. The lower suicidal ideation in Chennai was reported to be associated with the higher lethality of suicide attempts while in Durban the higher suicidal ideation rate was coupled with the moderate lethality of suicide attempts (Bertolote et al., 2005).

However, only few studies investigated the relationship between suicidal ideation and completed suicides. A multi-site survey which was conducted in several countries such as Canada, Germany, France, New Zealand and USA showed no clear association between suicide ideation rates and suicide mortality rates (Weisman et al., 1996). However, suicidal ideation rates were investigated in the general population whereas suicide mortality national rates were used for completed suicides. Therefore, the comparability of these data needs to be considered uncertain (Bertolote et al., 2010).

Further studies evaluated the importance of suicidal ideation as a predictor of suicidal behaviors, though this remains a highly debated question. Pirkis and colleagues (2001) showed that suicidal ideation may be considered a good predictor in the Australian general population of the utilization of health services, while Schweitzer and colleagues (1995) reported that over a half of those who attempted suicide in Australia did not use any mental health service before. Goldney and colleagues (1990) failed to confirm these results and raised doubts about the validity of suicidal ideation as a predictor of suicidal behaviors. Moreover, subjects who had previously acknowledged as having suicidal ideation denied it upon re-examination four years later (Goldney et al., 1990). Therefore, according to this point of view suicidal ideation would be a sign of distress rather than a long-term suicide outcome (Goldney et al., 1990). Finally, comparison of self-reported rates of suicidal ideation across groups may be complicated due to the nature of suicidal ideation which is often a fleeting, fluctuating experience that may be not clearly observable by others (WHO, 2014). Further studies investigating both the significance and prevalence of suicidal ideation are needed.

Risk Factors

Completed suicides as well as suicide attempts are complex phenomena determined by the interplay of different factors which interact in a complex network. Here, as follows we aimed to review some of the major risks factors related to suicidality.

Previous Suicide Attempts

One of the most relevant risk factors for the development of suicidal ideation is the presence of a positive history of previous suicide attempts. Overall, 40-55% of patients who attempted suicide had a history of prior suicide attempts (Rudd, 2006; Scoliers et al., 2009). A suicide attempt is associated with the risk of both additional suicide attempts (Owen et al., 2002) and completed suicides (Scoliers et al., 2009). Those who commit multiple suicide attempts –defined as “multiple attempters” - may be considered a cohort of patients who are at high suicide risk. The main characteristics of this group are: (1) female gender, (2) young age, (3) difficult socio-economic situation, (4) severe psychiatric disorders and comorbidity with other mental conditions (Groholt et al., 2009; Brezo et al., 2008; Courtet & Thuile, 2010; Osvath et al., 2003). Furthermore, this specific population has a high presence of suicide attempts or completed suicides in next of kin and this represents an independent risk factor for suicidal behaviors (Monin et al., 2012). Females are at higher risk to be hospitalized for repeated suicide attempts compared to males: this has been estimated to range approximately from1,2 (Chien et al., 2013) to 2,7 (Da Silva Cais et al., 2009) compared with the risk of male controls. However, a British study on multiple attempters reported no gender differences (Bennewith et al., 2002) while an Irish study showed suicide attempts to be higher in males, maybe linked with a widespread alcohol abuse in the local population (Corcoran et al., 2004). Among adolescents, common risk factors - apart from a positive history of suicide attempts in the family- substance abuse, history of sexual abuse, chronic medical conditions and psychotic disorders, which were predictive of another suicide attempt within a year from the first attempt occurrence (Vajda et al., 2000), may be considered. The frequency of repeated suicide attempts lowers with age (Chien et al., 2013; Bradvik et al., 2009). Concerning age, male multiple attempters are among aged20-35 years, while women aged 35 - 44 years old (Osvath et al., 2003). However, the majority of studies failed to show a significant age difference between single and multiple suicide attempters (Fullerton-Gleason, 2005). Moreover, males are more likely to repeat suicide attempts shortly after the previous one (Suominen et al., 2009). Particularly, 16% of the subjects reattempt suicide within a year (Owens et al., 2002). This percentage raises to 30% within the second year (Bille- Brahe et al., 2002) and remains unvaried until the fourth and fifth years from the first attempt (Kapur et al., 2006). Major depressive disorder, anxiety disorder, and substance abuse are among the most commonly encountered conditions in multiple suicide attempters (Monin et al., 2012). Moreover, major depressive disorder and substance abuse are notoriously correlated with suicide attempts and suicidal ideation (Bolton et al., 2010), while there are conflicting evidence about anxiety disorders. Some studies have not found any difference regarding anxiety disorders between suicide attempters and non- attempters (Goldston et al., 1998) while other studies seem to suggest significant correlations between panic attacks, post-traumatic stress disorder (PTSD), suicide attempts (Bolton et al., 2010; Krysinska et al., 2010), and repeated suicide attempts (Monin et al., 2012; Lopez- Castroman et al., 2011). Furthermore, multiple suicide attempters seem to have more often a history of clinically significant psychiatric disorders when compared with single suicide attempters. Major depressive disorders, anxiety disorders, substance abuse, and personality disorders, especially borderline personality disorders, were the most common conditions among multiple suicide attempters (Da Silva Cais et al., 2009; Scoliers et al., 2009

Giegling et al., 2009; Osvath et al., 2003). Studies that investigated differences in term of gender in multiple attempters showed that anxiety disorders, major depressive disorders, and PTSD were more common among females, whereas males had a more severe substance abuse, mainly alcohol, and were more often unemployed (Monin et al., 2012; Osvath et al., 2003). Concerning psychotic disorders there is no concluding evidence: some studies found that psychosis should be considered a risk factor among males multiple attempters (Osvath et al., 2003), while other studies reported hallucinations as significant risk factors among females multiple attempters (Kapur et al., 2006). These data suggested the necessity of organizing preventive strategies for multiple attempters based on gender (Monin et al., 2012).

Psychiatric Disorders

It has been estimated that at least 90% of completed suicides suffer from mental illness; furthermore, a diagnosis of any mental disorder enhances the risk of suicide by approximately 47-74% (Cavangh et al., 2003). Mood disorders, substance abuse, and substance-related disorders and personality disorders are among the most dangerous conditions for subsequent suicidal behaviors (Suominen et al., 1996).

Major depressive disorder is among the major risk factor for both completed and attempted suicides (Hawton &Van Heeringen, 2009). Evidence shows that depressed subjects were 20 times more likely to be at risk of suicidal behavior compared to healthy controls (Osby et al., 2001) and that 15% of depressed subjects have attempted suicide at least once in their life considering the non-clinical population (Malone et al., 1995) (in the clinically depressed subjects suicide attempts occurred in approximately 40% of the sample (Malone et al., 1995). Factors positively associated with a higher suicidal risk among depressed patients are: female gender (Osby et al., 2001), severe depressive symptoms (Roy, 2003), personal and family history of suicide attempts or completed suicides (Oquendo et al., 2007), comorbidity with anxiety disorders, personality disorders (Bolton et al.,2008), substance and alcohol abuse (Classen et al., 2007). Tobacco has been recognized to be a relevant risk factor for suicide in the depressed population due to the fact that depressed subjects who regularly smoke tobacco reported higher levels of impulsiveness and aggressiveness compared to depressed subjects who did not (Classen et al., 2007; Mann & Currier, 2010).

In subjects with bipolar disorder, a higher risk of suicide has been associated with rapid cycling, mixed states, mania with marked disphoric characteristics, and agitated depression (Wassermann et al., 2012; Rihmer, 2007), while suicidal behaviors seem more rare in mania with predominant euphoria (Rihmer, 2007). Moreover, an early onset and higher number of episodes resulted associated with higher risk for suicide, poor outcome, and impaired social functioning. In particular, the risk for suicidal behaviors was higher in the first years after the diagnosis of bipolar disorder as well as in the presence of a comorbidity with alcohol and other substances abuse (Rihmer, 2007).

The exact relationship between suicidal behaviors and anxiety disorders is not yet clear. Evidence shows a lifetime association between anxiety disorders, suicidal ideation, and suicide attempts among adolescents and young adults (Carter et al., 2003; Hill et al., 2011). However, some studies showed that this relationship among adolescents did not persist after controlling for major depression (Foley et al.,2006; Thompson et al., 2005). Conversely, anxiety traits such as chronic preoccupations and alarm, were significantly correlated with suicidal ideation and suicide attempts among young adults independently from the presence of major depression (Goldston et al., 2006). Among adults, PTSD and panic attacks were significantly associated with a higher risk of single (Bolton et al., 2008) and repeated suicide attempts (Monnin, 2012).

Alcohol and other substance abuse are among the major risk factors for suicidal ideation and behaviors both when present as single disorder and/or in comorbidity (Bolton et al., 2008; Krysinska et al., 2010). Males affected by substance abuse seem to be more likely to engage in suicidal behavior than females. Alcohol abuse may be associated with suicidal ideation and attempts in different ways, i.e. acute intoxication has been associated with sedation and thus it could be often used as self-medication by suicidal patients who were likely to seek relief from their sufferings (Wasserman et al., 2012). Furthermore, chronic alcohol abuse may facilitate brain deterioration leading to increased aggressiveness, impulsiveness, depression, and hopelessness (Wasserman et al., 2012). Hopelessness, a negative perspective regarding the future and described as playing a fundamental role in depression, may be also considered a key element throughout the suicidal process. Depression, and in particular hopelessness, may be considered as strong predictors of suicidal behavior (Pompili et al., 2011b, 2013).

More than 50% of suicide attempts in patients with chronic alcohol abuse are carried out during acute intoxication and are usually less severe compared to those carried out by depressed non abusers subjects. Suicidal ideation and suicidal planning could be reduced by the increase of impulsiveness related to the effects of alcohol (Suominen et al., 1996). Among substance abusers, opioid dependent abusers seem to have the higher risk for suicidal ideation and behaviors compared to stimulants and hallucinogens abusers (Maloney et al., 2007). In particular, a case-control study showed that 66% of opioid dependent abusers had ongoing suicidal ideation whereas among stimulant abusers, suicidal ideation was present in 55% of these subjects. Among opiate abusers, 31% had attempted suicide at least once in life (Maloney et al., 2007) and poli-abusers had an even higher risk for suicidal behaviors (Roy, 2002).

For what concerns eating disorders, a large study including a follow-up period of eight years showed that 15% of the subjects attempted suicide at least once during the study time frame. Of these subjects, 22% had a diagnosis of anorexia nervosa and 11% bulimia nervosa (Franko et al., 2004). Evidence showed that suicidal ideation and suicide attempts among subjects diagnosed with eating disorders were significantly associated with comorbid major depression, alcohol abuse, social phobia, and obsessive-compulsive disorder (Wasserman et al., 2012).

Schizophrenia patients had a significantly higher risk for suicidal ideation and suicide attempts compared to the general population. Suicidal thoughts and suicidal ideation had a particular pervasiveness in schizophrenia patients and evidence showed their presence in 30-50% of these patients (Meltzer, 2001). The rate "suicide attempts versus completed suicides" is significantly lower in this population and has been estimated to be approximately 5-10 suicide attempts for every completed suicide. This is presumably due to the use of more lethal methods to attempt suicide compared to other psychiatric populations (Barak et al., 2008). It has been estimated that 20-50% of schizophrenia patients attempt suicide at least once in their life (Meltzer, 2001) and 15% of patients also attempted suicide once before the first contact with mental health services (Addington et al., 2004). Moreover, a further 15% of schizophrenia suicide attempts occurred within the first five years after the first contact with mental health services (Addington et al., 2004). A Finnish study compared a large sample of schizophrenia patients hospitalized for a severe suicide attempts with a large group of patients hospitalized for a serious suicide attempts but without a psychiatric diagnosis. Schizophrenia patients had a significantly higher risk to reattempt suicide (58% of the group) and complete suicide (78%) compared to the other group without psychiatric diagnosis throughout the course of 3,6 follow-up period (Haukka et al., 2008). Being young, being male, having low social support and scarce treatment compliance, substance abuse, fear of mental disintegration, having multiple prior depressive episodes, and abundant positive symptoms were reported as factors predisposing to suicidality (Kelly et al., 2004; Hawton et al., 2005). Though a large body of literature attempted to differentiate suicidal schizophrenia patients from schizophrenics who were not at risk for suicide, evidence suggested that this is a still open debated question (Hawton et al., 2005). Though the communication of suicidal ideation and intent in schizophrenia is not simple due to its formal characteristics of thoughts and contents, evidence showed that in a sample of schizophrenia patients this communication resulted not significantly different compared to a group of non-psychotic patients (Heila & Lonnqvist, 2002). Subjects with first episodes psychosis (FEP) should be carefully evaluated for the presence of suicidal thoughts and suicidal ideation as there are studies showing that 21,6% of patients who attempted suicide and 4,3% who completed suicide carried out the act within the first seven years after the onset of psychosis (Robison et al., 2010). Among subjects who were more likely to attempt suicide early after the onset, being female and single, as well as having higher educational level have been suggested as specific risk factors for suicide (Levine et al., 2010). Furthermore, affective symptoms during FEP should be carefully evaluated as significant predictors of suicide (Robison et al., 2010).

Recently, the scientific community focused its attention on suicidality in adolescents diagnosed with pervasive developmental disorders (PDD). A Japanese group found that in a sample of 94 adolescents hospitalized for a suicide attempt, 12,4% had a diagnosis of PDD and showed a significantly lower presence of comorbid affective and anxiety disorders compared with adolescents without PDD formulated through the Autism – Spectrum Quotient Japanese version (AQ-J) (Mikami et al., 2009). Among pervasive developmental disorders, the most common Diagnostic and Statistical Manual (DSM) Fourth Edition Text Revision (TR) diagnosis among suicidal adolescents was Asperger Syndrome and PDD not otherwise specified (NOS) (Mikami et al., 2009). Overall, subjects diagnosed with Asperger Syndrome resulted more likely to engage in suicidal behaviors due to the better relational and social skills of this group compared with the other PDD. Asperger subjects may be more aware of their impairments and this would foster feelings of loneliness, isolation, and rejection despite the rigidity of thoughts. Evidence showed that Asperger subjects usually choose highly lethal methods to attempt suicide (Gillberg, 2002).

Personality Disorders have been often reported as comorbid conditions with DSM-IV TR axis I disorders among suicidal patients. Overall, 44% of suicidal patients reported an Axis I and Axis II comorbidity (Hawton et al.

2003) and 55-70% of subjects who attempted suicide at least once received one or more personality disorder (Schneider et al., 2008). Borderline personality disorder has been identified to be at higher risk to develop suicidality and evidence showed that 75% of those with borderline personality disorder attempted suicide at least once in life (Black et al., 2004). A history of childhood abuse – physical, sexual or both – and a diagnosis of PTSD significantly enhanced the risk of suicidal behavior among borderline subjects (Black et al., 2004). The high risk of suicidal behaviors in this group could be conceptualized in the light of the high impulsiveness and emotional dysregulation associated with this condition (Giegling et al., 2009). Antisocial and avoidant personality disorders have been significantly associated with a higher risk to develop suicidal ideation, though to a lesser extent if compared with borderline personality disorder (Duberstein et al., 2000). The study of suicidal behavior in subjects with personality disorders showed a higher frequency of negative life-events in the month before the suicide attempt; this could facilitate the gesture in the light of the scarce coping strategies, high aggressiveness, impulsiveness, hostility, anxiety, and primitive defense mechanisms of this population (Stanley et al., 2009).

Personality traits have been investigated in relationship with suicidality and evidence showed that anger, impulsiveness, and aggressiveness were among the most related dimensions to suicidality. Depressed women with suicidal ideation, history of violent or non- violent suicide attempts had significantly higher levels of aggressiveness and impulsiveness compared to non-suicidal depressed women (Giegling et al., 2009). Some authors (Mann et al., 2008; Oquendo et al., 2004) identified severe aggressiveness and depression as predictors of the development of suicidality in both males and females. Moreover, anger- related personality traits were often related with impulsiveness and aggressiveness in suicidal patients (Kirkcaldy et al., 2006) and impulsiveness, aggressiveness, and pessimism have been identified to significantly increase suicide risk after depressive episodes (Oquendo et al., 2004).

Studies concerning affective temperaments and personality traits showed that suicidal patients often had high levels of "novelty seeking" and "harm avoidance" together with lower "self-directedness" and "cooperativeness" when compared to non-suicidal patients (Giegling et al., 2009). A Canadian group reported an association between impulsive and aggressive personality traits that could form an impulsive-aggressive lifetime dimension significantly predisposing subjects to develop suicidality (McGirr & Turecki, 2007). However, when investigating the effects of impulsiveness on suicidal ideation, there are studies showing that younger subjects without psychiatric conditions were more likely to have higher impulsiveness and proceed from suicide ideation to suicide attempt without planning the gesture. Conversely, the presence of mental disorders and older age were more frequently associated with the progression from suicidal ideation to suicide attempts through suicidal plans (Levinson et al., 2007). Furthermore, the risk of progression from suicidal ideation to suicide attempts is higher in the first year after the onset of suicide ideation independently of impulsiveness levels (Levinson et al., 2007). The role of anger in the progression from suicide ideation to attempts through suicide plans is not so clear-cut. While certain studies showed that high levels of anger increased impulsiveness concerning the attempt (Jollant et al., 2005), other studies failed to confirm this result, in particular concerning the role of anger in the process of decision-making and suicidal planning (Martinotti et al., 2008).

Other Risk Factors

The exposure to a wide range of adverse life events has been significantly associated with an increased vulnerability to develop suicidal ideation and suicidal behaviors (Pompili et al., 2011a). In particular:

- Stressful life events during childhood, e.g. parents' separation and divorce; important family discord (Fergusson et al., 2000);
- History of childhood physical and/or sexual abuse (Molnar et al., 2001);
- Childhood neglect (Johnson et al., 2002);
- Low social support (Pompili et al., 2011a);
- Losses (e.g. grieves) and interpersonal conflicts that have been identified as important triggers for suicidal behaviors (Pompili et al., 2011a)

Studies that investigated the most important triggers for suicidal behaviors showed a significant interplay between childhood and adolescent stressful life events occurring in the months before the development of suicidality.

Stressful life events occurring in the six months before suicide attempts were more likely to be present among the subjects who attempt suicide for the first time compared to repeaters (88.8% *vs.* 78.7%) (Pompili et al., 2011a)

Subjects who repeatedly developed suicidal ideation and carried out repeated suicide attempts were more likely to have a history of early stressful life events and trauma (Pompili et al., 2011a), however there are studies that failed to confirm these results (Chandrasekaran et al., 2008). Both a single and cumulative lifetime effect has been hypothesized for the role of stressful life events in suicidal behavior. Pompili and colleagues (2011a) suggested that risk factors can either predispose to attempt suicide at an earlier age and, as a kindling phenomenon, determine a “suicide career” or, alternatively, an accumulation of stressors may produce a “last straw” effect. The kindling effect is used to describe diseases where each episode of the illness later enhances more frequent and severe episodes (Johnson et al., 2002). Similarly, risk factors may increase their strength each time the suicidal individual makes an attempt, and certain risk factors may come into play at a given time, even long after the suicide career has been developed. Conversely, in the case of the “last straw” effect, an accumulation of stressors is the central characteristic in determining suicide attempts (Pompili et al., 2011a).

Studies that investigated the role of early sexual abuse showed that it significantly increased the risk of suicidality, PTSD, major depressive disorder, impulsiveness, aggressiveness, and hostility not only in the abused victim but also in his offspring (Brodsky et al., 2008).

Sexual abuse appears to be more tightly related to suicidality than physical abuse (Anderson et al., 2002); furthermore, when comparing the offspring of physically abused victims and sexual abused victims, the offspring of the latter were at higher risk of suicidality and had higher impulsiveness, though presenting lower aggressiveness (Molnar et al., 2001). Sexual and physically victims may be also considered at higher risk of becoming suicidal (Anderson et al., 2002).

Finally, a strong relationship between psychiatric disorders, medical conditions such as cancer, diabetes mellitus, stroke, dementia, chronic headaches, multiple sclerosis, and suicidal behavior has been reported. Specifically, a strong association has been reported between primary headaches, psychiatric disorders, and suicidal behavior (Pompili et al., 2010); higher suicidal rates have been suggested in patients with multiple sclerosis compared with the general population (Pompili et al., 2012a); and stroke has been documented to confer a substantial risk for suicide (Pompili et al., 2012b).

Importantly, physical illness and chronic pain represent an important risk factor for suicide not only for the related physical pain and altered body function but also for the significant associated psychological distress (Jia et al., 2014).

Gene-Environment Interaction

Environment plays a pivotal role in modulating genes expression in early life stages, thus influencing the epigenome (Mann et al., 2003). Early traumatic events, physical, and sexual abuse may cause permanent alterations in genes expressions that later create a diathesis for psychiatric disorders (Szyf, 2009), suicidality (Evans et al., 2005), a specific reactivity to stress, impulsivity, and aggressiveness (Mann et al., 2003). Moreover, evidence shows that the prevalence of suicidal ideation and suicide attempts were positively related to both the degree and severity of the abuse (Fergusson et al., 2008; Brezo et al., 2008).

There is clear evidence that the activity of three neurobiological systems has a role in the pathophysiology of suicidal behavior. Specifically, the hyperactivity of the hypothalamic-pituitary-adrenal (HPA) axis, dysfunction of the serotonergic (5-HTergic) system, and excessive activity of the noradrenergic system may be significantly implicated. While the first and the last system appear to be involved in the response to stressful events, dysfunction of the serotonergic system has been hypothesized to be trait-dependent and associated with disturbances in the regulation of anxiety, impulsivity, and aggression. It can be postulated that neurobiological dysfunctions mediate the occurrence of suicidal behavior through the disturbed modulation of basic neuropsychological functions located in the prefrontal cortex (PFC) and limbic system (Van Heeringen, 2003). This explains the diathesis of suicidal subjects for major depression (Mann et al., 2010) and impulsive- aggressive traits (Giegling et al., 2009). Methylation is the epigenetic mechanism most relevantly associated with early trauma and was able to cause the silencing of certain genes by preventing the binding of transcription factors to DNA (Labonte & Turecki, 2010). Childhood neglect early mother separation and physical abuse have been significantly associated with alterations of genes involved in the serotonergic system, such as the serotonin receptor 1A and 1B (5HT1A; 5HT1B); the serotonin transporter (SERT); tryptophan hydroxylase (TPH); serotonin-transporter-linked polymorphic region (5-HTTLPR); monoamine oxidase A (MAO-A) both in humans and rodents (Van Heeringen, 2003). Animal studies showed that even small differences in early maternal care may cause different gene methylation in the hippocampus (Champagne et al., 2008) and that early maternal separation may cause a decreased functioning of the serotonergic system, that is determined by the presence of the short variant of the promoter of serotonin transporter (5-HTTLPR-S) (Uher & McGuffin, 2007). The 5-HTTLPRS-S in humans is associated with an increased risk for major depression, aggression, and suicide attempts in adulthood (Uher & McGuffin, 2007).

A considerable body of literature shows the relationships between aggression, increased reactivity to stressors, emotional dysregulation, suicidal behavior and two or three tandem repetition variants of MAO-A (2R-MAO-A; 3R-MAO-A) (Bortolato et al., 2013). Childhood abuse and early neglect may mediate the relationship between 2R- and 3R- MAO, aggression (Bortolato et al., 2013) and suicidality in males (Huang et al., 2004). Studies of functional brain imaging showed that the 3R variant was significantly associated with both structural and functional alterations in the orbito-frontal cortex (OFC) and limbic system as well as the hyper-reactivity of the amigdala and hippocampus during tasks of recalling negative life – events (Hung et al., 2012). However, the association between MAO-A variants and suicidality may be considered controversial (Courtet et al., 2005).

Moreover, a considerable inhibition of the BDNF hippocampal production and its receptor tropomyosin receptor kinase B (TrkB) in response to the exposure to acute and chronic stressors has been reported. This may induce impairments in the development of serotonergic system (Sher, 2011) as well as increased risk of suicidal ideation and behaviors in adolescence (Pandey et al., 2008). However, dysfunctions of the serotonergic system seem to be associated only with a diathesis for aggressiveness and suicidality and not with pathological behaviors resulting from a complex interplay between environmental and gene-related factors. The interplay of these variables may induce impairments in emotional regulation and social skills due to altered circuits in the prefrontal cortex, limbic areas, and raphe nucleus, which determine a diathesis for auto- and hetero-aggressive behaviors under distress (Bortolato et al., 2013).

Studies investigating the involvement of HPA-axis and noradrenergic system in suicidal behaviors reported the existence of a hypersensitivity to stressors among subjects with a positive history of suicide attempts. Childhood abuse and early neglect have been associated with the hyper-reactivity of the HPA-axis with an altered level of neuropeptide Y and corticotropic releasing factor (CRF) (Heim & Nemeroff, 2001) that have been shown to be related with a higher risk of suicidality (Mann, 2003; Pompili, 2010). Subjects with previous suicide attempts had significantly higher values of urinary cortisol in a 24-hour sample compared to subjects who never attempted suicide (Van Heeringen, 2003).

The heritability of suicidal behaviors and suicidality has been estimated to range from 17% to 45%. Studies showed that subjects who had a history of suicide in the family were at a significantly higher risk for suicide compared to subjects without such a history; these results have been confirmed also after being corrected for the presence of psychiatric disorders (Brent et al., 2008). Endophenotypes have been investigated to explain the occurrence of certain behaviors and related genetic variants in suicidal families. The endophenotypes suggested to be related to suicidal behaviors are:

a. Impulsive and aggressive traits: high levels of impulsivity and aggression are associated with a higher risk to develop suicidality and suicidal behaviors (Oquendo et al., 2004) with highly lethal methods (Placidi et al., 2001). Aggression is a dimensional trait with a heritability of almost 40-47% (Mann et al., 2009). Family studies showed a co segregation of the impulsive/aggressive endophenotype and suicidality (Melhem et al., 2007) and a relationship between impulsivity/aggression with certain genetic variants related to the serotonergic system such as 5-HT2A; 5-HT1B e MAO-A (Mann et al., 2009). Impulsive traits have been associated with 5-HT2A in subjects with alcohol abuse (Mann et al., 2009).
b. Early onset of depression: studies showed the association between early onset of depression and increased risk for suicidality and suicide attempts (Mann et al., 2009). The Sequenced Treatment Alternatives to Relieve Depression Study (STAR*D) demonstrated a triple risk of suicide attempts among subjects who had the onset of depression before the age of 18 compared to subjects who had this onset in an older age (Zisook et al., 2007). Linkage studies showed an association of alterations in the chromosomal loci 15q, 17p,8p and 6p (Holmans et al., 2007) among subjects who had the first episode before the age of 18 compared to subjects who had the first episode later (Zisook et al., 2007). Linkage studies showed an association between early onset of depression, suicidality, and chromosome variants which were localized in 15q, 17p, 8p, and 6p (Holmans et al., 2007).
c. Neurocognitive functions: evidence showed a considerable number of neurocognitive alterations among suicidal subjects. Subjects who attempted suicide using highly lethal methods had significant deficits in selective attention compared to subjects who attempted suicide

using less lethal methods. Furthermore, this may be directly related to impairments in focusing attention and problem-solving tasks (Keilp et al., 2008). Subjects who repeatedly attempt suicide had deficits in focusing attention (Wenzel et al., 2009). These neurocognitive impairments have been shown to have an heritability of 39-50% (Mann et al., 2009) and there is contrasting evidence concerning its relationship with the heritability with depressive disorders (Reppermund et al., 2009; Westheide et al., 2008).

d. Cortisol response to psycho-social stressors: evidence reported that alterations in the HPA-axis were associated to higher suicidality (Mann et al., 2009). Early traumatic events have been proven to be related to a hyperactive response of the HPA axis to psychosocial stressors as well as to particular polymorphisms of mineralocorticoid and glucocorticoid receptors (DeRijk et al., 2008), 5-HTTLPR-S (Gotlib et al., 2008), and the alpha 6 GABA-A receptors(Oquendo et al., 2003).

Moreover, recent studies suggested the existence of additional biological variants that could be considered endophenotypes for suicidal behaviors though it is still uncertain whether these variables fulfill the required criteria to be really considered endophenotypes (Dwivedi et al., 2004; Dwivedi and Pandey, 2011). Further studies are needed to investigate the role of other biological variables, such as brain structure (Dwivedi et al., 2004), and brain metabolism (Dwivedi & Pandey, 2011) in influencing suicidality and identifying further possible endophenotypes.

Psychometric Assessment

The use of psychometric scales for the assessment and measurement of suicidal dimension has acquired a growing interest in the scientific community for clinical research and forensic purposes. Despite the large number of rating scales validated to investigate different aspects of suicidality, this chapter focuses only on those instruments concerning suicidal ideation that were proven to be clinically consistent by functional analyses as proposed by Emmelkamp (2004). According to this model, validated rating scales were analyzed through a micro- and macro-analysis where the former focused on the suicidal behavior as a process and the latter on the external factors of an instrument that may be relevant for the prediction of the suicidal risk

(Emmelkamp, 2004). Thus, the validity assessed through this model essentially refers to the clinical validity of a scale (Bech & Awata, 2009). Moreover, the reliability of psychometric scales depends on their administration including both the rater's attitude and knowledge of the scale (often raters and administrators have to complete specific training programs in order to effectively use certain instruments) and the environment where the administration and rating have been performed. This enhances not only the inter-raters reliability but also the possibility to compare different studies using the same tool, and the reliability of single evaluations for clinical purposes (Bech & Awata, 2009).

Furthermore, suicidal ideation can be investigated through specific scales or, alternatively as reported throughout some studies, through items included in other scales such as the Hamilton Depression Rating Scale (HAM-D, Beck et al., 1986) and the Paykel's Clinical Interview for Depression (CID, Paykel, 1985).

HAM-D (Beck et al., 1986) contains a single item (item 3) that investigates suicidal ideation. When used separately from the scale, item 3 had an inter-rater reliability coefficient of 0,92 (Reynolds, 1991) and its predictive validity was assessed in a study showing that patients who scored 2 or higher were 4,9 times (95% confidence interval 2,7-9.0) more likely to commit suicide than patients who scored less than 2 (Brown, 2004). CID (Paykel, 1985) contains a single item referring to suicidal tendencies, that was also validated in a single standing version - The Suicidal Ladder (Paykel et al., 1974), which is a five-item hierarchy of questions addressing to the single components of the suicidal process. In other words, this scale follows the performance of mounting a ladder that leads to suicide attempt. This was reported in the Paykel's study (1974) showing that 3,5% of the subjects felt that life was not worth living: 2,8% wished themselves dead; 1,0% had thoughts of taking their life and 0,6% had made a suicide attempt over the past year. This confirmed that the five items of the Scale are additive according to Faravelli's perspective (Faravelli, 2004), i.e. the individual item can be rank-ordered consistently according to its relation to the severity of the suicidal process. This implies that scoring of lower prevalence items presupposes scorings on higher prevalence items, thus mirroring the processuality of suicidality.

However, the most frequently used scale with more than five items to measure suicidal ideation is the Scale for Suicidal Ideation (SSI, Beck et al., 1979). This instrument contains 19 items, each of which can be scored 0 to 2 with the theoretical total score ranging from 0 to 38. Higher scores have been correlated with more suicidal thoughts. The original version covers current suicidal ideation, though variants referring to past ideation have been developed (Bech & Awata, 2009). Its inter-rater reliability is adequate and the internal consistency is apparently high (Cronbach's coefficient alpha 0,89). However, this coefficient depends on the number of items and is not an expression of additivity in Faravelli's sense (Feinstein, 1987). However, Beck and colleagues (Beck et al., 1999) subsequently published the SSI including a measure of suicidal thoughts at the worst point of the patient's life (SSI-W). Patients who scored in the high risk category were over 10 times more likely to commit suicide than patients scoring in the low risk category. The SSI-W has also been found significantly associated with the suicidal item (item 3) of the HDRS (Brown, 2004).

The Columbia Suicide Severity Rating Scale (C-SSRS, Posner et al., 2011) rates the individual's degree of suicidal ideation, ranging from "wish to be dead" to "active suicidal ideation with specific plan and intent." Subjects presenting a single behavior identified by the scale were 8 to 10 times more likely to commit suicide (Posner et al., 2011). The C-SSRS includes 4 subscales: Suicidal Ideation; Intensity of Ideation; Suicidal Behaviors, and Actual Attempts. The internal consistency of the C-SSRS was examined at two assessment intervals: since last visit and past week and was high (Cronbach's alpha 0.937) to moderate (Cronbach's alpha 0.73). This was also confirmed in a sample of adolescents (Posner et al., 2011).

PREVENTION

Traditionally, there are three levels of suicide prevention, namely universal, selective and indicated prevention (Mrazek & Haggerty, 1994). These kinds of prevention target different populations:

- *Universal prevention:* refers to activities targeting the general population, including health promotion and education for early risk identification. It aims to reduce the number of suicides fostering prevention nets within the population;
- *Selective prevention:* focuses on vulnerable subjects at high risk for suicide, who however did not report suicidal ideation nor behaviors. This kind of prevention is aimed to decrease risk factors and foster well-being;

- *Indicated prevention:* focuses on suicidal subjects such as psychiatric patients reporting suicidal ideation or planning.

Though mental illness has been estimated in at least 90% of completed suicides (Cavangh et al., 2003), studies focusing on suicide prevention strategies suggested the importance of a multidisciplinary approach to suicide in order to develop effective prevention programs. Though different prevention strategies have been developed to address particular populations such as adolescents and old subjects, a milestone for suicide prevention remains a thorough attention on the environment that can overthrow feelings of loneliness, isolation, and disconnection potentially triggering suicidal behaviors. Moreover, interventions of public education seek to reduce stigmatization of mental illness and suicide challenging the acceptance of suicide as inevitable or an appropriate solution of life problems, including serious medical disorders. However, the effectiveness of these interventions in the general population are difficult to evaluate (Mann et al., 2005). Furthermore, there are several studies that assessed the role of community-based gatekeeper programmes that aimed to train specific community figures, such as teachers, clergy, pharmacists, geriatric caregivers in suicide prevention so that they could help in the identification and referral of at risk subjects. However, no concluding evidence of the effectiveness of these figures has been provided (Mann et al., 2005). Pompili and Tatarelli (2010) identified some relevant guidelines that may be applied by community caregivers to be helpful to subjects threatening suicide. Specifically, they recommend:

1. To be aware of the risk and learn the most relevant warning signs;
2. To get involved and be available showing interest and support;
3. To ask tactfully about suicidal thoughts;
4. To be direct and talk openly and freely about suicide;
5. To be willing to listen, allow and accept the expression of feelings;
6. To be non-judgmental and not debate whether suicide is right or wrong, or whether the feelings are good or bad – such as lecturing on the value of life;
7. Don't dare him/her to do it.

The *Harvard Medical School Guide to Suicide Assessment and Intervention* underlines how "every effort should be made to integrate mental health services provision with the existing health and social service systems" (Jacobs, 1999, p.69). In particular, prevention in primary care with a specific training in suicide prevention of non-mental health professionals such as general practitioners and nurses should be carried out. Studies showed that up to 83% of suicides had a contact with a primary care physician within one year before their death and 66% in the month before suicide (Mann et al., 2005). Key prevention strategies in primary care include an improved screening and treatment of depressed patients (Mann et al., 2005). Therefore, a multidisciplinary network promoting mental health in parallel with early recognition of warning signs and social support strategies should be constructed to develop effective prevention strategies (Varnik, 2014).

The *International Association for Suicide Prevention* (IASP) together with the *American Association of Suicidology* (AAS) currently stress the importance of creating "connections among people" (Arensman, 2014) both in the sense of micro-connections between individuals at a community level, researchers, and macro-connections (i.e. international connections among suicide prevention groups). This could allow moving from individual actions to national suicide prevention programs involving government and policy representative in an ongoing dialogue. The World Health Association (WHO, 2014) launched the World Suicide Report (WSR) in 2014 that follows the adoption of the WHO- Comprehensive Mental Health Action Plan 2013-2020 which commits all member states to reduce their suicide rates of 10% by 2020, but suicide prevention still remains a global imperative for which further developments and understandings are undoubtedly needed (WHO, 2014).

REFERENCES

Addington, J., Williams, J., Young, J., Addington, D. Suicidal behaviour in early psychosis. *Acta Psych. Scand.,* 2004; 109(2): 116-20.

Aghanwa, H. S. The characteristics of suicide attempters admitted to the main general hospital in Fiji Islands. *J. Psychosom. Res.*, 2000; 49: 439- 445.

Alem, A., Kebede, D., Jacobsson, L., Kullgren, G. Suicide attempts among adults in Butajira, Ethiopia. *Acta Psych. Scand.*, 1999; 397: 70-6.

Anderson, P. L., Tiro, J. A., Price, A. W., Bender, M. A., Kaslow, N. J. Additive impact of childhood emotional, physical, and sexual abuse on suicide attempts among low-income African American women. *Suicide Life Threat. Behav.,* 2002; 32(2): 131–138.

Angst, J., Clayton, P.J. Personality, smoking and suicide: a prospective study. *J. Affect.Disord.,*1998; 51: 55–62.

Australian Bureau of Statistics. The health and welfare of Australia's aboriginal and Torre Strait Islander People. *Australian Bureau of Statistics, Camberra*. Retrived online,2005; http://www.abs.gov.au/a 2005.

Baraff, L. J., Janowicz, N., Asarnow, J. R. Survey of California emergency departments about practices for management of suicidal patients and resources available for their care. *Ann. Emerg. Med.,* 2006; 48: 452-8.

Barak, Y., Baruch, Y., Achiron, A., Aizenberg, D. Suicide attempts of schizophrenia patients: A case-controlled study in tertiary care. *J. Psych. Res.,* 2008; 42: 822-26.

Barr W., Leitner M., Thomas J. Psychosocial assessment of patients who attend an accident and emergency department with self-harm. *J. Psychiatr. Ment. Health Nurs.,* 2005; 12: 130-8.

Beautrais, A. L. Suicides and serious suicide attempts in youth: a multiple-group comparison study. *Am. J. Psychiatry*, 2003; 160: 1093–99.

Bech, P., Awata, S. Measurement of suicidal behavior with psychometric scales. In: Wassermann D., Wassermann C. ed., *Oxford Textbook of Suicidology and Suicide Prevention*. Oxford: Oxford University Press 2009.

Bekry, A. A. Trends in suicide, parasuicide and accidental poisoning in Addis Ababa, Ethiopia. Ethiop. *J. Health Dev.,* 1999; 13(3): 247-62.

Bennewith, O., Stocks, N., Gunnell, D., Peters, T. J., Evans, M. O., Sharp, D. J. General practice based intervention to prevent repeat episodes of deliberate self-harm: cluster randomized controlled trial. *B.M.J.*, 2002; 324: 1254-57.

Bertolote, J. M. Suicide in the world: an epidemiological overview 1959-2000. In: Wassermann D. ed., *Suicide an unnecessary death*. London: Martin Dunitz 2001.

Bertolote, J. M., Wasserman D. Developments of definitions of suicidal behaviours. In: *Oxford Textbook of Suicidology and Suicide Prevention*. Oxford: Oxford University Press 2009.

Bertolote, J. M., Fleischmann, A., De Leo, D., Bolhari, J., Botega, N., De Silva, D., et al. Suicide attempts, plans, and ideation in culturally diverse sites: the WHO SUPRE-MISS community survey. *Psychol. Med.*, 2010 35(10): 1457-65.

Bille-Brahe, U., Kerkhof, A. J. F. M., Leo, D. D., Schmidtke, A., Crepet, P. Lönnqvist, J., et al. A repetition-prediction study of European parasuicide populations: a summary of the first report from Part I1 of the WHO/EURO Multicentre Study on Parasuicide in co-operation with the

EC Concerted Action on Attempted Suicide. *Acta Psychiatr. Scand.*, 1997; 95: 81-86.

Bille-Brahe, U., Schmidtke, A., Kerhof, A. Background and introduction to the study. In: Kerkhof A., Schmidtke A., Bille- Brahe U. eds, *Attempted suicide in Europe. Findings from the Multicentre Study on Parasuicide by the WHO Regional Office for Europe*, pp. 3- 15. Leiden: DSWO Press 1964.

Black, D. W., Blum, N., Pfohl, B., Hale, N. Suicidal behavior in borderline personality disorder: prevalence, risk factors, prediction, and prevention. *J. Pers. Disord.*, 2004; 18(3): 226-239.

Bolton, J. M., Belik, S. L., Enns, M. W., Cox, B. J., Sareen, J. Exploring the correlates of suicide attempts among individuals with major depressive disorder: findings from the national epidemiologic survey on alcohol and related conditions. *J. Clin. Psychiatry*, 2008; 69: 1139–49.

Bolton, J. M., Pagura, J., Enns, M. W., Grant, B., Sareen, J. A population based longitudinal study of risk factors for suicide attempts in major depressive disorder. *J. Psychiatr. Res.,* 2010; 44(13): 817–26.

Bortolato, M., Pivac, N., Seler, D. M., Nikolac Perkovic, M., Pessia, M., Di Giovanni, G. The role of the serotonergic system at the interface of aggression and suicide. *Neuroscience*, 2013; 236: 160-85.

Botega, N. J., Barros, M. B., Oliveira, H. B., Dalgalarrondo, P., Marín-León, L. Suicidal behavior in the community: prevalence and factors associated with suicidal ideation. *Rev. Bras. Psiquiatr.*, 2005; 27(1): 45-53.

Bradvik, L., Berglund, M. Repetition and severity of suicide attempts across the life cyrcle: a comparison by age group between suicide victims and controls with severe depression. *B.M.C. Psychiatry*, 2009; 9:62-72.

Brent, D. A., Melhem, N. Familial transmission of suicidal behavior. *Psych. Clin. North Am.*, 2008; 31(2): 157-77.

Brent, D. A., Moritz, G. Developmental pathways to adolescent suicide. In: D. Chichetti, S. Toth (Eds.), *Adolescents: opportunities and challenges*. New York: University of Rochester Press 1996.

Brezo, J., Paris, J., Hébert, M., Vitaro, F., Tremblay, R., Turecki, G. Broad and narrow personality traits as markers of one-time and repeated suicide attempts: a population-based study. *B.M.C. Psychiatry*, 2008; 8: 5-11.

Brickman, A. L., Mintz, D. C. US rates of self-inflicted injuries and suicide, 1992–1999. *Psych. Serv.*, 2003; 54(2): 168-73.

Brodsky, B. S., Mann, J. J., Stanley, B., Tin, A., Oquendo, M., Birmaher, B., et al. Familial transmission of suicidal behavior: factors mediating the relationship between childhood abuse and offspring suicide attempts. *J. Clin. Psychiatry*, 2008; 69(4), 584.

Brown, G. K., Jeglic, E., Beck, A. T. Cognitive Therapy, Cognition, and Suicidal Behavior. In: Ellis ed.: *Cognition and suicide: theory, research and therapy*. Washington: American Psychological Association 2006.

Canetto, S. S. Meanings of gender and suicidal behaviour during adolescence. *Suicide Life Threat. Behav.*, 1997; 27 (4): 339-51.

Carter, T. D., Mundo, E., Parikh, S. V., Kennedy, J. L. Early age at onset as a risk factor for poor outcome of bipolar disorder. *J. Psychiatr. Res.*, 2003; 37:297–303.

Cavanagh, J.T.O., Carson, A. J., Sharpe, M., Lawrie, S. M. Psychological autopsy studies of suicide: a systematic review. *Psychol. Med.*, 2003;33: 395–405.

CDC (Center for disease control and prevention). *Youth Risk Behaviour Surveillance – USA 2011*.MMWR, 2012; 61 (4), 8th June 2012.

CDC (Centers for Disease Control and Prevention). Suicide and Attempted Suicide - China, 1990-2002 Morbidity and Mortality Weekly Report 53; 481-484 retrieved online on 7 April 2013 at http://www.cdc.gov/mmwR /preview/mmwrhtml/mm5322a6.htm 2004.

Champagne, D. L., Bagot, R. C., van Hasselt, F., Ramakers, G., Meaney, M. J., De Kloet, E. R., et al. Maternal care and hippocampal plasticity: evidence for experience-dependent structural plasticity, altered synaptic functioning, and differential responsiveness to glucocorticoids and stress. *J. Neuroscience*, 2008; 28(23): 6037-45.

Chandrasekaran, R., Gnananselane, J. Predictors of repeat suicidal attempt after first-ever attempt: a two-year follow-up study. *Hong Kong J. Psychiatry*, 2008; 18:131-135.

Chen, P. C., Lee, L. K., Wong, K. C., Kaur, J. Factors relating to adolescent suicidal behavior: a cross-sectional Malaysian school survey. *J. Adolesc. Health*, 2005; 37(4): 11-337.

Cheung, Y. B., Law, C. K., Chan, B., Liu, K. Y., Yip, P. S. Suicidal ideation and suicidal attempts in a population-based study of Chinese people: risk attributable to hopelessness, depression, and social factors. *J. Affect. Disord.,* 2006; 90(2-3): 193-99.

Chien, W. C., Lai, C. H., Chung, C. H. A nation- wide evidence- based analysis of repeated suicide attempts. *Crisis*, 2013; 34(1): 22-31.

Christiansen, E., Frank Jensen, B. Risk of repetition of suicide attempt, suicide or all deaths after an episode of attempted suicide: a register-based survival analysis. *Australasian Psych*., 2007; 41(3): 257-65.

Claassen, C. A., Trivedi, M. H., Shimizu, I., Stewart, S., Larkin, G. L., Litovitz, T. Epidemiology of nonfatal deliberate self-harm in the United States as described in three medical databases. *Suicide Life Threat. Behav*., 2006; 36: 192-212.

Claassen, C. A., Trivedi, M. H., Rush, A. J., Husain, M. M., Zisook, S., Young, E. Clinical differences among depressed patients with and without a history of suicide attempts: findings from the STAR*D trial. *J. Affect. Disord.,* 2007; 97:77–84.

Corcoran, P., Keeley H. S., O'Sullivan, M., Perry, I. J. The incidence and repetition of attempted suicides in Ireland. *Eur. J. Public Health*, 2004; 14 (1): 19-23.

Courtet, P., Thuile, J. *Les suicidants multirécidivistes: une population particulère? Suicides et tentatives de suicide*. Paris: Médecine-Sciences Flammarion, pp. 26–31, 2010.

Courtet, P., Jollant, F., Buresi, C., Castelnau, D., Mouthon, D., Malafosse, A. The monoamine oxidase A gene may influence the means used in suicide attempts. The monoamine oxidase A gene may influence the means used in suicide attempts. *Psychiatr. Genet.*, 2005; 15(3): 189-93.

Crumlish, N., Whitty, P., Kamali, M., Clarke, M., Browne, S., McTigue, O., et al. Early insight predicts depression and attempted suicide after 4 years in first-episode schizophrenia and schizophreniform disorder. *Acta Psych. Scand.,* 2005; 112:449–55.

Da Silva Cais, C. F., Stefanello, S., Fabrício Mauro, M. L., Vaz Scavacini de Freitas, G., Botega, N. J. Factors associated with repeated suicide attempts. Preliminary results of the WHO Multisite Intervention Study non Suicidal Behavior (SUPRE-MISS) from Campinas, Brazil. *Crisis*, 2009; 30: 73–8.

De Leo, D., Milner, A., Sveticic, J. Mental Disorders and Communication of Intent to Die in Indigenous Suicide Cases, Queensland, Australia. *Suicide Life Threat. Behav.,* 2012; 42(2): 57-64.

De Leo, D., Burgis, S., Bertolote, J. M., Kerkhof, A. J., Bille-Brahe, U. Definitions of suicidal behavior. *Crisis*, 2006; 27(1): 4-15.

Deisenhammer, E. A., Strauss, R., Kemmler, G., Hinterhuber, H., Weiss, E. M. The duration of the suicidal process: how much time is left for intervention between consideration and accomplishment of a suicide attempt? *J. Clin. Psychiatry*, 2009; 70(1): 19-24.

Dejong, T.M., Overholser, J. C., Stockmeier, C.A. Apples to oranges?: A direct comparison between suicide attempters and suicide completers. *J. Affect. Disord.,* 2010; 124: 90–97.

Deonarain, M., Pillay, B. J. A study of parasuicide behaviour at the Chris Hani Baragwanath Hospital. *Suicid. Behav.*, 2000; 4: 112-27.

DeRijk, R. H., van Leeuwen, N., Klok M. D., Zitman, F. G. Corticosteroid receptor-gene variants: Modulators of the stress-response and implications for mental health. *Eur. J. Pharmacol.*, 2008; 585 (2–3): 492-501.

Duberstein, P. R., Conwell, Y., Seidlitz, L., Denning, D. G., Cox, C., Caine, E. D. Personality traits and suicidal behavior and ideation in depressed inpatients 50 years of age and older. *J. Gerontol. B. Psychol. Sci. Soc. Sci.*, 2000; 55:18–26.

Dwivedi, Y., Pandey, G. N. Elucidating biological risk factors in suicide: Role of protein kinase A. *Prog. Neuropsychopharmacol. Biol. Psych.*, 2011; 35(4): 831-41.

Dwivedi, Y., Rizavi, H. S., Conley, R. R., Roberts, R. C., Tamminga, C. A., Pandey, G. N. Altered gene expression of brain-derived neurotrophic factor and receptor tyrosine kinase B in postmortem brain of suicide subjects. *Arch. Gen. Psychiatry*, 2004; 60(8): 804-15.

Emmelkamp, P. M. The additional value of clinimetrics needs to be established rather than assumed. *Psychother. Psychosom.*, 2004; 73(3): 142-144.

Evans, E., Hawton, K., Rodham, K. Suicidal phenomena and abuse in adolescents: a review of epidemiological studies. *Child Abuse Negl.*, 2005; 29(1): 45-58.

Fergusson, D. M., Boden, J. M., Horwood, L. J. Exposure to childhood sexual and physical abuse and adjustment in early adulthood. *Child Abuse Negl.*, 2008; 32(6): 607-19.

Fergusson, D. M., Woodward, L. J., Horwood, L. J. Risk factors and life processes associated with the onset of suicidal behaviour during adolescence and early adulthood. *Psychol. Med.*, 2000; 30: 23–39.

Fleischmann, A., Bertolote, J. M., De Leo, D., Botega, N., Phillips, M., Sisask, M., et al. Characteristics of attempted suicides seen in emergency care settings of general hospitals in eight low and middle income countries. *Psychol. Med.*, 2005; 35(10): 1467- 1474.

Foley, D. L., Goldston, D. B., Costello, E. J., Angold, A. Proximal psychiatric risk factors for suicidality in youth: The Great Smoky Mountains study. *Arch. Gen. Psychiatry,* 2006; 63(9): 1017–24.

Franko, D. L., Keel, P. K., Dorer, D. J. Blais, M. A., Delinsky, S. S., Eddy, K. T., et al. What predicts suicide attempts in women with eating disorders? *Psychol. Med.*, 2004; 34: 843-53.

Freeman, D. J., Wilson, K., Thigpen, J., McGee, R. K. Assessing intention to die in self-injury behavior. *Psychol. Assess. Suicid. Risk*, 1974; 494: 18-30.

Fullerton-Gleason, L. *Suicide surveillance in Colorado. Analysis of hospital discharge data: Identifying characteristics associated with a second hospitalized suicide attempt*. Denver: The Injury Epidemiology Program, Colorado Department of Public Health and Environment 2005.

Fushimi, M., Sugawara, J., Saito, S. Comparison of completed and attempted suicide in Akita, Japan. *Psychiatr. Clin. Neurosci.,* 2006; 60: 289–95.

Giegling, I., Olgiati, P., Hartmann, A. M., Calati, R., Möller, H. J., Rujescu, D. Personality and attempted suicide. Analysis of anger, aggression and impulsivity. *J. Psychiatr. Res*., 2009; 43: 1262–71.

Gillberg, C. *A guide to Asperger syndrome*. London: Cambrige University Press 2002.

Gmitrowicz, A., Szymczak, W., Kotlicka-Antczak, M. Suicidal ideation and suicide attempt in Polish adolescents: is it a suicidal process?. *Int. J. Adolesc. Med. Health*, 2003; 15(2): 113-24.

Goldney, R. D., Smith, S., Winefield, A. H., Tiggeman, M., Winefield, H. R. (1991). Suicidal ideation: its enduring nature and associated morbidity. *Acta Psych. Scand*., 83(2): 115-120.

Goldston, D. B., Daniel, S. S., Reboussin, B. A., Reboussin, D. M., Kelley, A. E., Frazier, P. H. Psychiatric diagnoses of previous suicide attempters, first-time attempters, and repeat attempters on an adolescent inpatient psychiatry unit. *J. Am. Acad. Child Adolesc. Psych*., 1998; 37: 924–32.

Goldston, D. B., Reboussin, B. A., Daniel, S. S. Predictors of suicide attempts: State and trait components. *J. Abnorm. Psychol*., 2006; 115(4): 842–849.

Gotlib, I. H., Joormann, J., Minor, K. L., Hallmayer, J. HPA-Axis reactivity: A mechanism underlying the associations among 5-HTTLPR, stress, and depression. *Biol. Psychiatry.,* 2008; 63(9): 847-851.

Gottesman, I. I., Gould, T. D. The endophenotype concept in psychiatry: etymology and strategic intentions. *Am. J. Psychiatry*., 2005; 160(4): 636-45.

Groholt, B., Ekeberg, O. Prognosis after adolescent suicide attempt: mental health, psychiatric treatment, and suicide attempts in a nine year follow-up study. *Suicide Life Threat. Behav*., 2009; 39: 125–136.

Haukka, J., Suominen, K., Partonen, T., Lönnqvist, J. Determinants and outcomes of serious attempted suicides: a nationwide study in Finland from 1996-2003. *Am. J. Epidemiol*., 2008; 67(10): 1155-63.

Hawton, K., Arensman, E., Wasserman, D., Hulten, A., Bille-Brahe, U., Bjerke T., et al. Relation between attempted suicides and suicide rates among young people in Europe. *J. Epidemiol. Comm. Health*, 1998; 52: 191- 94.

Hawton, K., Zahl D., Weatherall, R. Suicide following deliberate self-harm: long-term follow-up of patients who presented to a general hospital. *Br. J. Psichiatry*, 2003; 182: 537-42.

Hawton, K. Completed suicides after attempted suicides: methods used in attempts may indicate the degree of risk. *B. M. J.*, 2010; 341: 158-9.

Hawton, K., Sutton, L., Haw, C., Sinclair, J., Deeks, J. J. Schizophrenia and suicide: systematic review of risk factors. *Br. J. Psichiatry,* 2005; 187(1): 9-20.

Hawton, K., Van Heeringen, K. Suicide. *Lancet,* 2009; 373: 1372-81.

Head, L, Campbell-Hewson, G. L., O'Keane, V. No harm done? Psychological assessment in the A&E department of patients who deliberately harm themselves. *J. R. Coll. Physicians Lond.*, 1999; 33:51-5.

Health Canada. *Unintentional and intentional injury profile for aboriginal people in Canada.* Health Canada, Ottawa. Online: http://www.hc-sc.gc.ca/index-eng.php 2001.

Heila, H., Lonnqvist, J. The clinical epidemiology of suicide in schizophrenia. In: Murray R., Jones P., Susser E., Van Os, J., Cannon, M., eds., *The Epidemiology of Schizophrenia*, pp. 288-316. Cambridge University Press: Cambridge 2002.

Heim, C., Nemeroff, C. B. The role of childhood trauma in the neurobiology of mood and anxiety disorders: preclinical and clinical studies. *Biol. Psychiatry*, 2001; 49(12): 1023-39.

Helps, Y., Harrison J. Hospitalized injury of Australia's aboriginal and Torres Strait Islander People. *A.I.H.W. catalogue.* 2006; 94.

Hesketh, T., Ding, Q. J., Jenkins, R. Suicide ideation in Chinese adolescents. *Soc. Psychiatry Psychiatr. Epidemiol.*, 2002; 37: 230–5.

Hill, R. M., Castellanos, D., Pettit, J. W. Suicide-related behaviors and anxiety in children and adolescents: A review. *Clin. Psychol. Rev.*, 2011; 31(7): 1133-44.

Holmans, P., Weissman, M. M., Zubenko, G. S., Scheftner, W. A., Crowe, R R., DePaulo Jr. Genetics of recurrent early-onset major depression (GenRED): final genome scan report. *Am. J. Psychiatry*, 2007; 164(2): 248-58.

Horesh, N., Levi, Y., Apter, A. Medically serious versus non-serious suicide attempts: Relationships of lethality and intent to clinical and interpersonal characteristics. *J. Affect. Disord.,* 2012; 136(3): 286-93.

Huang, Y. Y., Cate, S. P., Battistuzzi, C., Oquendo, M. A., Brent, D., Mann, J. J. An association between a functional polymorphism in the monoamine oxidase a gene promoter, impulsive traits and early abuse experiences. *Neuropsychopharmacol.*, 2004; 29: 1498-505.

Hung, C. F., Lung, F. W., Hung, T. H., Chong, M. Y., Wu, C. K., Wen, J. K., et al. Monoamine oxidase A gene polymorphism and suicide: an association study and meta-analysis. *J. Affect. Disord.,* 2012; 136(3): 643-49.

Inoue, K., Tanii, H., Fukunaga, T., Abe, S., Nishimura, F., Kimura, Y., et al. The importance of the frequency of suicide attempts as a risk factor of suicide. *J. Forensic Leg. Med.*, 2008; 15: 24–26.

Isometsä, E. T., Henriksson, M. M., Aro, H. M., Heikkinen, M. E., Kuoppasalmi, K. I., Lönnqvist, J. K. Suicide in major depression. *Am. J. Psychiatry*, 1994; 151: 530–6.

ISTAT Nota informativa "*I suicidi in Italia: tendenze e confronti, come usare le statistiche*" 08 agosto 2012. Accessibile online: www.istat.it 2012.

Jacobs, D., Douglas, G. *The Harvard Medical School guide to suicide assessment and intervention*. Jossey-Bass, 1999.

Jia, C. X., Wang, L. L., Xu, A. Q., Dai, A. Y., Qin, P. Physical illness and suicide risk in rural residents of contemporary China: a psychological autopsy case-control study. *Crisis*, 2014; 35(5): 330-7.

Johnson, R. L., Thomas, R. G., Thomas, K. E. *State Injury Indicators Report*, Third Edition–2004 Data Centers for Disease Control and Prevention, National Center for Injury Prevention and Control, Atlanta retrieved online on 07 April 2013 at: http://www.cdc.gov/injury/stateprograms/indicators_2004.html.

Johnson, J. G., Cohen, P., Gould, M. S., Kasen, S., Brown, J., Brook, J. S. Childhood adversities, interpersonal difficulties, and risk for suicide attempts during late adolescence and early adulthood. *Arch. Gen. Psychiatry*, 2002; 59: 741–749.

Joiner, Jr., T. E., Rudd, M. Intensity and duration of suicidal crises vary as a function of previous suicide attempts and negative life events. *J. Consult. Clin. Psychol.*, 2000; 68: 909–16.

Jollant, F., Bellivier, F., Leboyer, M., Astruc, B., Torres, S., Verdier, R., et al. Impaired decision making in suicide attempters. *Am. J. Psychiatry*, 2005; 162(2): 304-10.

Joseph, A., Abraham, S., Muliyil, J. P., George, K., Prasad, J., Minz, S., et al. Evaluation of suicide rates in rural India using verbal autopsies, 1994–1999. *B. M. J.,* 2003;326: 1121–2.

Kapur, N., Cooper, J., King-Hele, S., Webb, R., Lawlor, M., Rodway, C., Appleby, L. The repetition of suicidal behavior: a multicenter cohort study. *J. Clin. Psychiatry*, 2006; 67: 1599–609.

Kattimani, S., Bharadwaj, B., Sarkar, S., Mukherjee, A. Interrater Reliability of the Silverman., et al. Nomenclature for Suicide-Related Ideations, Behaviors, and Communications. *Crisis*, 2015; 36(1): 61-64.

Kebede, D., Alem, A. Suicide attempts and ideation among adults in Addis Ababa, Ethiopia. *Acta Psych. Scand.*, 1999; 397: 35-9.

Keilp, J. G., Gorlyn, M., Oquendo, M. A., Burke, A. K., Mann, J. J. Attention deficit in depressed suicide attempters. *Psychiatr. Res*., 159: 7-17.

Kelly, D. L., Shim, J. C., Feldman, S. M., Yu, Y., Conley, R. R. Lifetime psychiatric symptoms in patients with schizophrenia who died by suicide compared to others means of death. *J. Psychiatr. Res*., 2004; 38: 531-6.

Kerkhof, A. J., Bernasco, W., Bille-Brahe, U., Platt, S., Schmidtke, A. *European parasuicide study interview schedule (EPSIS*). Facts and figures: WHO/EURO.

Kessler, R. C., Borges, G., Walters, E. E. Prevalence of and risk factors for lifetime suicide attempts in the National Comorbidity Survey. *Arch. Gen. Psychiatry*, 1999; 56: 617-26.

Kienhorst, C. W. M., de Wilde, E. J., van den Bout, J., Broese van Groenou, M. I., Diekstra, R. F., Wolters, W. H. G. Self-Reported Suicidal Behavior in Dutch Secondary Education Students. *Suicide Life Threat. Behav*., 1990; 20(2): 101-13.

Kinyanda, E., Hjelmeland, H., Musisi, S. Deliberate self-harm as seen in Kampala, Uganda-a case control study. *Soc. Psychiatry Psychiatr. Epidemiol,*. 2004; 39: 318-25.

Kirkcaldy, B. D, Siefen, G. R., Urkin, J., Merrick, J. Risk factors for suicidal behavior in adolescents. *Minerva Pediatr,* 2006; 58:443–50.

Kjoller, M., Norlev, J., Davidsen, M. *Recall bias and suicidal behavior in a six year follow-up study. In 10th European Symposium on Suicide and Suicidal Behaviour.* Copenhagen, Denmark: National Institute of Public Health 2004.

Kreitman, N. Parasuicide. *Br. J. Psychiatry*, 1969; 115 (523):747-56.

Krysinska, K., Lester, D. Post-traumatic stress disorder and suicide risk: a systematic review. *Arch. Suicide Res*., 2010; 14: 1–23.

Kumar, C.T., Mohan, R., Ranjith, G., Chandrasekaran, R. Gender differences in medically serious suicide attempts: A study from South India. *Psychiatr. Res.,* 2006; 144: 79–86.

Labonte, B., Turecki, G. The epigenetics of suicide: explaining the biological effects of early life environmental adversity. *Arch. Suicide Res*., 2010; 14(4): 291-310.

Laloë, V. Patterns of deliberate self-burning in various parts of the world: A review. *Burns*, 2004; 30 (3): 207-15.

Leenaars, A. *Suicide Notes*. Human Sciences Press, New York 1988.

Levi, Y., Horesh, N., Fischel, T., Treves, I., Or, E., Apter, A. Mental pain and its communication in medically serious suicide attempts: an "impossible situation." *J. Affect. Disord.,* 2008; 111: 244–50.

Levine, S.Z., Bakst, S., Rabinowitz, J. Suicide attempts at the time of first admission and during early course schizophrenia: a population based study. *Psychiatry Res*., 2010; 177: 55–9.

Levinson, D., Haklai, Z., Stein, N., Polakiewicz, J., Levav, I. Suicide ideation, planning and attempts: results from the Israel National Health Survey. *Isr. J. Psychiatry,* 2007; 44(2): 136-43.

Lewinsohn, P. M., Rohde, P., Seeley, J. R., Baldwin, C. L. Gender differences in suicide attempts from adolescence to young adulthood. *J. Am. Acad. Child Adolesc. Psych.,* 2001; 40: 427–34.

Liu X., Tein J.Y., Zhao Z., Sandler I. N. Suicidality and correlates among rural adolescents of China. *J. Adolesc. Health*, 2005; 37: 443–51.

Lopez-Castroman, J., de las Mercedes Perez-Rodriguez, M., Jaussent, I., Alegria, A. A., Artes-Rodriguez, A., Freed, P., et al. Distinguishing the relevant features of frequent suicide attempters. *J. Psychiatr. Res*., 2011; 45: 619–25.

Lucero Abreu, R. K., Díaz Romero, N., Villalba, L. Caracterización clínica y epidemiológica de los suicidios en Montevideo y de los intentos de autoeliminación (IAE) en el Hospital de Clínicas en el período abril 2000-abril 2001: el método de la autopsia psicológica; Clinical features and epidemiology of suicides in Montevideo and suicide attempts at the Hospital de Clinicas from april 2000 to april 2001. *Rev. Psiquiatr. Uruguay,* 2003; 67(1): 5-20.

McCauley, M., Russell, V., Bedford, D., Khan, A., Kelly, R. Assessment following deliberate self-harm: who are we seeing and are we following the guidelines? *Ir. J. Psych. Med*., 2001; 18: 116-9.

Madu, S. N., Matla, M. P. The prevalence of suicidal behaviours among secondary school adolescents in the Limpopo Province, South Africa. *S. Afr. J. Psychol.,* 2003; 133: 126-32.

Malone, K. M., Szanto K., Corbitt, E. M., Mann, J. J. Clinical assessment versus research methods in the assessment of suicidal behavior. *Am J Psychiatry,* 1995; 152: 1601-7.

Maloney, E., Degenhardt, L., Darke, S., Mattick, R. P., Nelson, E. Suicidal behavior and associated risk factors among opioid- dependent individuals: a case- control study. *Addiction,* 2007; 102: 1033-41.

Mann J.J., Currier D. M. Stress, genetics and Epigenetics effects in the neurobiology of suicidal behavior and depression. *Eur Psychiatry,* 2010; 25 (5): 268-71.

Mann, J. J. Neurobiology of suicidal behaviour. *Nat Rev Neurosci,* 2003; 4(10): 819-28.

Mann, J. J., Apter, A., Bertolote, J., Beautrais, A., Currier, D., Haas, A., et al. Suicide prevention strategies: a systematic review. *JAMA*., 2005; 294(16): 2064-74.

Mann, J. J., Arango, V. A., Avenevoli, S., Brent, D. A., Champagne, F. A., Clayton, P., et al. Candidate endophenotypes for genetic studies of suicidal behavior. *Biol Psychiatry,* 2009; 65(7): 556-63.

Mann, J. J., Ellis, S. P., Waternaux, C. M., Liu, X., Oquendo, M. A., Malone, K. M., et al. Classification trees distinguish suicide attempters in major psychiatric disorders: a model of clinical decision making. *J. Clin. Psychiatry,* 2008; 69(1): 23-31.

Manuck, S. B., Flory, J. D., Ferrell, R. E., Mann, J. J., Muldoon, M. F. A regulatory polymorphism of the monoamine oxidase-A gene may be associated with variability in aggression, impulsivity, and central nervous system serotonergic responsivity. *Psychiatry Res*., 2000; 96: 9-23.

Maris, R. W. Suicide. *Lancet,* 2002; 360: 319–26.

Martinotti, G., Mandelli, L., Di Nicola, M., Serretti, A., Fossati, A., Borroni, S., et al. Psychometric characteristic of the Italian version of the Temperament and Character Inventory—Revised, personality, psychopathology, and attachment styles. *Compr. Psychiatry,* 2008; 49(5): 514-22.

Mboussou, M., Milebou-Aubusson, L. Suicides and attempted suicides at the Jeanne Ebori Foundation, Libreville (Gabon)]. *Med. Trop. (Mars)*, 1989; 49(3): 259-67.

McGirr, A., Turecki, G. The relationship of impulsive aggressiveness to suicidality and other depression-linked behaviors. *Curr. Psychiatry Rep.,* 2007; 9(6): 460-66.

McGirr, A., Renaud, J., Bureau, A., Seguin, M., Lesage, A., Turecki, G. Impulsive-aggressive behaviours and completed suicide across the life cycle: a predisposition for younger age of suicide. *Psychol. Med.,* 2008; 38(3): 407-17.

McKenzie, K., van Os, J., Samele, C., Van Horn, E., Tattan, T., Murray, R. Suicide and attempted suicide among people of Caribbean Origin with psychosis living in the UK. *Br. J. Psychiatry,* 2003; 183: 40-4.

Melhem, N. M., Brent, D. A., Ziegler, M., Iyengar, S., Kolko, D., Oquendo, M., et al. Familial pathways to early-onset suicidal behavior: familial and individual antecedents of suicidal behavior. *Am. J. Psychiatry.,* 2007; 164(9): 1364-70.

Meltzer H.Y. Treatment of suicidality in schizophrenia. *Ann. N Y. Acad. Sc.,* 2001; 932:44–58.

Mikami, K., Inomata, S., Hayakawa, N., Ohnishi, Y., Enseki, Y., Ohya, A., et al. Frequency and clinical features of pervasive developmental disorder in adolescent suicide attempts. *Gen. Hosp. Psychiatry,* 2009; 31: 163–6.

Ministry of Health. *Suicide Facts: 2010 data*. Ministry of health, Wellington, retrieved online: www.health.govt.nz/publication/suicide-facts-deaths-and-intentional-self-harm-hospitalisations-2010.

Miret, M., Nuevo, R., Morant, C., Sainz-Cortón, E., Jiménez-Arriero, M. Á., López-Ibor, J. J., et al. Quality of written information about suicide attempts. *Rev. Psiquiatr. Salud Mental,* 2010; 3(1): 13-8.

Molnar, B. E., Berkman, L. F., Buka, S. L. Psychopathology, childhood sexual abuse and other childhood adversities: relative links to subsequent suicidal behaviour in the US. *Psychol. Med.,* 2001; 31: 965–77.

Monnin, J., Thiemard, E., Vandel, P., Nicolier, M., Tio, G., Courtet, P., et al. Sociodemographic and psychopathological risk factors in repeated suicide attempts: Gender differences in a prospective study. *J. Affect. Disord.,* 2012;136(1): 35-43.

Mrazek, P. J., Haggerty, R. J. (Eds.) *Reducing the risk for mental disorder: Frontiers for prevention intervention research*. Washington, DC: National Academy Press, Institute of Medicine 1994.

Nishi, D., Matsuoka, Y., Kawase, E., Nakajima, S., Kim, Y. Mental health service requirements in a Japanese medical centre emergency department. *Emerg. Med. J.,* 2006; 23(6): 468-69.

Nordentoft, M, Sogaard, M. Registration, psychiatric evaluation and adherence to psychiatric treatment after suicide attempt. *Nord. J. Psychiatry,* 2005; 59: 213-6.

Nordström, P., Samuelsson, M., Åsberg, M. Survival analysis of suicide risk after attempted suicide. *Acta Psychiatr. Scand.,* 1995; 91(5): 336-40.

Nwosu, S. O., Odesanmi, W. O. Pattern of suicides in Ile-Ife, Nigeria. *West Afr. J. Med,.* 2001; 20: 259-62.

O'Carroll, P. W. Attempted suicide among young adults: progress toward a meaningful estimate of prevalence. *Am. J. Psychiatry,*1992; 149: 41-55.

O'Carroll, P. W., Berman, A. L., Maris, R. W., Moscicki, E. K., Tanney, B. L., Silverman, M. M. Beyond the Tower of Babel A nomenclature for suicidology. *Suicide Life Threat. Behav,* 1996; 26: 237–52.

Odejide, A. O., Williams, A. O., Ohaeri, J. U., Ikuesan, B. A. The epidemiology of deliberate self-harm. The Ibadan experience. *Br. J. Psychiatry,* 1986; 149: 734-37.

Okasha, A., Lotaif, F. Attempted suicide. An Egyptian investigation. *Acta Psychiatr. Scand.,* 1979; 60(1): 69-75.

Oquendo, M. A., Bongiovi-Garcia, M. E., Galfalvy, H., Goldberg, P. H., Grunebaum, M. F., Burke, A. K., et al. Sex differences in clinical predictors of suicidal acts after major depression: a prospective study. *Am. J. Psychiatry,* 2007; 164:134–41.

Oquendo, M. A., Galfalvy, H., Russo, S., Ellis, S. P., Grunebaum, M. F., Burke, A., Mann, J. J. Prospective study of clinical predictors of suicidal acts after a major depressive episode in patients with major depressive disorder or bipolar disorder. *Am. J. Psychiatry*, 2004; 161(8): 1433-41.

Oquendo, M. A., Placidi, G. P., Malone, K. M., Campbell, C., Keilp, J., Brodsky, B., et al. Positron emission tomography of regional brain metabolic responses to a serotonergic challenge and lethality of suicide attempts in major depression. *Arch. Gen. Psychiatry,* 2003; 60(1): 14-23.

Ösby, U., Brandt, L., Correia, N., Ekbom, A., Sparén, P. Excess mortality in bipolar and unipolar disorder in Sweden. *Arch. Gen. Psychiatry* 2001; 58:844–50.

Osváth, P., Kelemen, G., Erdös, M. B., Vörös, V., Fekete, S. The main factors of repetition: review of some results of the Pecs Center in the WHO/EURO Multicentre Study on Suicidal Behaviour. *Crisis,* 2003; 24: 151-154.

Ovuga, E., Boardman, J., Wasserman, D. Integrating mental health into primary health care: local initiatives from Uganda. *World Psychiatry,* 2007; 6(1): 60-71.

Owens, D., Horrocks, J., House, A. Fatal and non-fatal repetition of self-harm. Systematic review. *Br. J. Psychiatry,* 2002; 181: 193–99.

Pandey, G. N., Dwivedi, Y., Rizavi, H. S., Teppen, T., Gaszner, G. L., Roberts, R. C., Conley, R. R. GSK-3β gene expression in human postmortem brain: regional distribution, effects of age and suicide. *Neurochem. Res.,* 2009; 34(2): 274-85.

Pandey, G. N., Ren, X., Rizavi, H. S., Conley, R. R., Roberts, R. C., Dwivedi, Y. Brain-derived neurotrophic factor and tyrosine kinase B receptor signalling in post-mortem brain of teenage suicide victims. *Int. J. Neuropsychopharmacology.,* 2008; 11(8): 1047-53.

Pelser, D. J. W., Oberholzer, D. J. *Attempted suicide (parasuicide*), Medunsa/Ga-Rankuwa Hospital, South Africa. 1987; 14: 22-4.

Pirkis, J., Beautrais, A., Durkee, T. Suicide attempts in New Zealand and Australia. In: Wassermann D., Wassermann C. ed., *Oxford Textbook of Suicidology and Suicide Prevention*. Oxford: Oxford University Press 2009.

Pirkis, J. E., Burgess, P. M., Meadows, G. N., Dunt, D. R. Suicidal ideation and suicide attempts as predictors of mental health service use. *Med. J. Austr., 2001;* 175(10): 542-5.

Placidi, G. P., Oquendo, M. A., Malone, K. M., Huang, Y. Y., Ellis, S. P., Mann, J. J. Aggressivity, suicide attempts, and depression: relationship to cerebrospinal fluid monoamine metabolite levels. *Biol. Psychiatry,* 2001; 50: 783-91.

Pompili, M., Serafini, G., Di Cosimo, D., Dominici, G., Innamorati, M., Lester, D., et al. Psychiatric comorbidity and suicide risk in patients with chronic migraine. *Neuropsychiatr. Dis. Treat.*, 2010; 6: 81-91.

Pompili, M., Innamorati, M., Szanto, K., Di Vittorio, C., Conwell, Y., Lester, D., et al. Life events as precipitants of suicide attempts among first-time suicide attempters, repeaters, and non-attempters. *Psychiatry Res.,* 2011a; 186: 300–5.

Pompili, M., Iliceto, P., Luciano, D., Innamorati, M., Serafini, G., Del Casale, A., et al. Higher hopelessness and suicide risk predict lower self-deception among psychiatric patients and non-clinical individuals. *Riv. Psichiatr.,* 2011b; 46(1): 24-30.

Pompili, M., Forte, A., Palermo, M., Stefani, H., Lamis, D.A., Serafini, G., et al. Suicide risk in multiple sclerosis: a systematic review of current literature. *J. Psychosom. Res.*, 2012a; 73(6): 411-7.

Pompili, M., Venturini, P., Campi, S., Seretti, M. E., Montebovi, F., Lamis, D. A., et al. Do stroke patients have an increased risk of developing suicidal ideation or dying by suicide? An overview of the current literature. *CNS Neurosci. Ther.*, 2012b; 18(9): 711-21.

Pompili, M., Innamorati, M., Gonda, X., Serafini, G., Sarno, S., Erbuto, D., et al. Affective temperaments and hopelessness as predictors of health and social functioning in mood disorder patients: a prospective follow-up study. *J. Affect. Disord.*, 2013; 150(2): 216-22.

Pompili, M., Tatarelli, R. *Evidence-based practice in Suicidology*. Gottingen: Hoegrefe 2010.

Pompili, M. Exploring the phenomenology of suicide. *Suicide Life Threat. Behav.,* 2010; 40: 234–44.

Posner, K., Brown, G. K., Stanley, B., Brent, D. A., Yershova, K. V., Oquendo, M. A., et al. The Columbia–Suicide Severity Rating Scale: initial validity and internal consistency findings from three multisite studies with adolescents and adults. *Am. J. Psychiatry*, 2011; 168(12): 1266-1277.

Post, R.M., Transduction of psychosocial stress into the neurobiology of recurrent affective disorder. *Am. J. Psychiatry,*1992; 149 (5): 999–1010.

Ramberg, I. L. *Promoting suicide prevention. An evaluation of a program for training trainers in psychiatric clinical work.* Doctoral Thesis, Karolinska Instituet, Stockholm 2003.

Ramberg, I. L., Wasserman, D. Prevalence of reported suicidal behaviour in the general population and mental health-care staff. *Psychol. Med*, 2000; 30(5): 1189-96.

Rancāns, E., Lapiņš, J., Renberg, E. S., Jacobsson, L. Self-reported suicidal and help seeking behaviours in the general population in Latvia. *Soc. Psychiatry Psychiatr. Epidemiol.*, 2003; 38(1): 18-26.

Reppermund, S., Ising, M., Lucae, S., Zihl, J. Cognitive impairment in unipolar depression is persistent and non-specific: further evidence for the final common pathway disorder hypothesis. *Psychol. Med.*, 2009; 39(4): 603-14.

Rihmer, Z. Suicide risk in mood disorders. *Curr. Opin. Psychiatry*, 2007; 20: 17–22.

Robinson, J., Harris, M. G., Harrigan, S. M., Henry, L. P., Farrelly, S., Prosser, A., et al. Suicide attempt in first-episode psychosis: a 7.4-year follow-up study. *Schizophr. Res,* 2010; 116: 1–8.

Robson, B., Purdie, G., Cram, F., Simmonds, S. Age standardisation–an indigenous standard?. *Emerg. Themes Epidemiol.*, 2007; 4(1): 3-15.

Roy, A. Characteristics of opiate dependent patients who attempt suicide. *J. Clin. Psychiatry*, 2002; 63: 403-7.

Roy, A. Features associated with suicide attempts in depression: a partial replication. *J. Affect. Disord.,* 2003; 27: 35–8.

Rudd, M. D. Suicidality in clinical practice: Anxieties and answers. *J. Clin. Psychol.*, 2006; 62(2): 157-9.

Schlebusch L., Burrows S. Suicide attempts in Africa. In: Wassermann D., Wassermann C. ed , *Oxford Textbook of Suicidology and Suicide Prevention*. Oxford: Oxford University Press 2009.

Schlebusch, L. *Suicidal behaviour in South Africa.* Pietermaritzburg, University of KwaZulu-Natal Press 2005.

Schmidtke, A., Bille-Brahe, U., DeLeo, D., Kerkhof, A., Bjerke, T., Crepet, P., et al. Attempted suicides in Europe: rates trends and sociodemographic characteristics of suicide attempters during the period 1989- 1992. Results of the WHO/EURO Multicentre study on parasuicide. *Acta Psychiatr. Scand.*, 1996; 93: 127-338.

Schmidtke, A., Bille- Brahe, U., De Leo, D. *Suicidal behavior in Europe: results from the WHO/ EURO multicenter study on suicidal behavior.* Goettingen: Hoegrefe and Huber 2001.

Schneider, B., Schnabel, A., Wetterling, T., Bartusch, B., Weber, B., Georgi, K. How do personality disorders modify suicide risk?. *J. Pers. Disord.*, 2008; 22(3): 233-45.

Schweitzer, R., Klayich, M., McLean, J. Suicidal ideation and behaviours among university students in Australia. *Aust. NZ. J. Psychiatry*, 1995; 29(3): 473-479.

Scoliers, G., Portzky, G., Van Heeringen, K., Audenaert, K. Sociodemographic and psychopathological risk factors for repetition of attempted suicide: a 5- year follow-up study. *Arch. Suicide Res.*, 2009; 13: 201- 13.

Sheidman, E. *Suicide as psycheache: a clinical approach to self-destructive behavior*. Jason Aronson Inc.: Northvale.

Sher, L. Brain-derived neurotrophic factor and suicidal behavior. *Q. J. M.*, 2011;104(5): 455-58.

Shneidman, E. S. *Definition of suicide*. Northvale, NJ: Jason Aronson 1985.

Silverman, M. M., Berman, A. L., Sanddal, N. D., O'Carroll, P. W., Joiner, T. E. Rebuilding the. tower of babel: A revised nomenclature for the study of suicide and suicidal behaviors Part 1: Background, rationale, and methodology. *Suicide Life Threat. Behav.,* 2007a; 37(3): 248-63.

Silverman, M. M., Berman, A. L., Sanddal, N. D., O'Carroll, P. W., Joiner, T. E Rebuilding the Tower of Babel: A Revised Nomenclature for the Study of Suicide and Suicidal Behaviors Part 2: Suicide-Related Ideations,

Communications, and Behaviors. *Suicide Life Threat. Behav.*, 2007b; 37(3): 264-77.

Sinclair, J. M., Harriss, L., Baldwin, D. S., King, E. A. Suicide in depressive disorders: a retrospective case-control study of 127 suicides. *J. Affect. Disord.*, 2005; 87: 107-13.

Stanley, B., Jones, J. Risk for suicidal behaviour in personality disorders. In: Wasserman D, Wasserman C, editors. *Oxford textbook of suicidology and suicide prevention: a global perspective*. Oxford: Oxford University Press; 2009.

Stengel, E. *Suicide and attempted suicide*. Baltimore: Penguin Books 1964.

Suokas, J., Lonnqvist, J. Outcome of attempted suicide and psychiatric consultation: risk factors and suicide mortality during a five year follow-up. *Acta Psychiatr. Scand.*, 2001; 84: 545-9.

Suominen, K., Henriksson, M., Suokas, J., Isometsä, E., Ostamo, A., Lönnqvist, J. Mental disorders and comorbidity in attempted suicide. *Acta Psychiatr. Scand.*, 1996; 94: 234–40.

Suominen, K., Haukka, J., Valtonen, H. M., Lonnqvist, J. Outcome of patients with major depressive disorder after serious suicide attempt. *J. Clin. Psychiatry*, 2009; 70: 1372–8.

Szyf, M. The early life environment and the epigenome. *Biochimica et Biophysica Acta (BBA)-General Subjects*, 2009: 1790(9): 878-85.

Thompson, E. A., Mazza, J. J., Herting, J. R., Randell, B. P., Eggert, L. L. The mediating roles of anxiety, depression, and hopelessness on adolescent suicidal behaviors. *Suicide Life Threat. Behav.*, 2005; 35(1): 14–34.

Uhart, M., McCaul, M. E., Oswald, L. M., Choi, L., Wand, G. S. GABRA6 gene polymorphism and an attenuated stress response. *Mol. Psychiatry*, 2004; 9(11): 998-1006.

Uher, R., McGuffin, P. The moderation by the serotonin transporter gene of environmental adversity in the aetiology of mental illness: review and methodological analysis. *Mol. Psychiatry*, 2007; 13(2): 131-46.

Vajda, J., Steinbeck, K. Factors associated with repeat suicide attempts among adolescents. *Austr. NZ. J. Psychiatry*, 2000; 34(3): 437-45.

Van Heeringen, K., Hawton, K., Williams, J. M. G. Pathways to suicide; an integrative approach. In: K. Hawton, K. van Heeringen (Eds.), *The International Handbook of Suicide and Suicidal Behaviour*, Wiley, Chichester , 2000, pp. 223–234.

Van Heeringen, K. The neurobiology of suicide and suicidality. *Can. J. Psychiatry*, 2003; 48 (5): 292- 300.

Varnik, A. *International Association for Suicide Prevention Newsbulletin*, August/September 2014.

Vishnuvardhan, G., Saddichha, S. Psychiatric comorbidity and gender differences among suicide attempters in Bangalore, India. *Gen. Hosp. Psychiatry*, 2012; 34: 410–14.

Wagner, B. M., Wong, S. A., Jobes, D. A. Mental health professionals' determinations of adolescent suicide attempts. *Suicide Life Threat. Behav.*, 2002; 32(3): 284-300.

Wasserman, D., Rihmer, Z., Rujescu, D., Sarchiapone, M., Sokolowski, M., Titelman, D., et al. The European Psychiatric Association (EPA) guidance on suicide treatment and prevention. *Eur. Psychiatry*, 2012; 27:129–41.

Wasserman, D. (Ed.). *Suicide: an unnecessary death.* New York: Taylor & Francis, 2001.

Wei, S., Yan, H., Chen, W., Liu, L., Bi, B., Li, H., et al. Gender-specific differences among patients treated for suicide attempts in the emergency departments of four general hospitals in Shenyang, China. *Gen. Hosp. Psychiatry*, 2013; 35: 54–8.

Weissman, M. M., Bland, R. C., Canino, G. J., Faravelli, C., Greenwald, S., Hwu, H. G., et al. Cross-national epidemiology of major depression and bipolar disorder. *J.A.M.A.*, 1996; 276(4): 293-9.

Weissman, M. M., Bland, R. C., Canino, G. J., Greenwald, S., Hwu, H. G., Joyce, P. R., et al. Prevalence of suicide ideation and suicide attempts in nine countries. *Psychol. Med.*, 1999; 29(1): 9-17.

Wenzel, A., Brown, G., Beck, A. *Cognitive Therapy for Suicidal Patients*. Washington DC: APA Books. 2009.

Westheide, J., Quednow, B. B., Kuhn, K. U., Hoppe, C., Cooper-Mahkorn, D., Hawellek, B., et al. Executive performance of depressed suicide attempters: the role of suicidal ideation. *Eur. Arch. Psychiatry Clin. Neurosci.,* 2008; 258(7): 414-21.

World Health Organization, *Preventing Suicide: a Global imperative*. Luxemburg: WHO, 2014.

Wyder, M., De Leo, D. Behind impulsive suicide attempts: indications from a community study. *J. Affect. Disord.*, 2007; 104(1): 167-73.

Yamamura, T., Kinoshita, H., Nishiguchi, M., Hishida, S. A perspective in epidemiology of suicide in Japan. *Vojnosanitetski pregled*, 2006; 63(6): 575-83.

Youth Violence Prevention Center Under the Microscope: *Asian and Pacific Islander Youth in Oakland Needs, Issues, Solutions Published by the National Council on Crime and Delinquency*, Oakland, Calif., August

2007. Retrieved 07 April 2013 at: http://www.yvpcenter.org/media/docs/9167_UndertheMicroscopeUpdate2007_online.pdf 2003.

Zhang, K. R., Han, X. M, Ma, H. X. Adolescent suicidal ideation and correlates. *Chin. J. Clin. Psychol.*, 1998; 6: 181–2.

Zisook, S., Rush, A. J., Lesser, I., Wisniewski, S. R., Trivedi, M., Husain, M. M., et al. Preadult onset vs. adult onset of major depressive disorder: a replication study. *Acta Psychiatr. Scand.*, 2007; 115(3): 196-205.

Zubin, J. Observations on nosological issues in the classification of suicidal behavior. In: Beck A.T., Resnik H.L.P., Lettieri D.J. ed., *The Psychotherapic Prediction of suicide*, pp. 3-25. Bowie: Charles Press Publishers 1974.

In: Suicidal Ideation
Editor: Bradley Weaver
ISBN: 978-1-63483-092-8

Chapter 2

SUICIDAL SYMPTOMS AMONG VETERANS WITH CHRONIC PTSD EVALUATED FOR TREATMENT AT A VA HOSPITAL

Jack R. Cornelius, Jon D. Walker, Gloria Klima and Barry Fisher

V.I.S.N. 4 Mental Illness Research, Education and Clinical Center (M.I.R.E.C.C.), V.A. Pittsburgh Healthcare System, Pittsburgh, PA, US

1. INTRODUCTION

Since 2001, more than 2.2 million American Veterans have served in Afghanistan (Operation Enduring Freedom, or OEF) and in Iraq (Operation Iraqi Freedom, or OIF) (Sayer, 2011). PTSD is the most frequently diagnosed mental disorder among OIF/OEF Veterans seeking care through the Department of Veterans Affairs (Seal, Bertenthal, Miner, Sen, & Marmar, 2007, and the current prevalence of PTSD among military veterans is estimated at 8% (Institute of Medicine, 2014). The prevalence rate for suicide in the US military has increased substantially since 2005 (LeardMann et al., 2014; Nock et al., 2014). Data from the National Comorbidity Study (NCS) demonstrated that PTSD is independently associated with suicide attempts in the general population (adjusted odds ratio =1.81; 95% CI: 1.45 - 2.26) (Nepon et al., 2010). PTSD has also been shown to predict completed suicides among military veterans (Bullman & Kang, 1994; Schoenbaum et al., 2013).

Recent studies have demonstrated that PTSD is a significant risk factor for suicidal ideation in Iraq and Afghanistan War Veterans (Jakupcak et al., 2009; Pietrzak et al., 2010; Guerra et al., 2011), and for suicide attempts (Oquendo et al., 2003) and for completed suicide in the general population (Gradus et al., 2010). PTSD has been shown to be associated with an increased risk of suicidal ideation even among PTSD diagnosed persons who are not dually diagnosed with either MDD or AUD (Guerra et al., 2011). Thus, PTSD and PTSD-related suicidality are pressing current public health concerns among veterans and non-veterans (Seal et al., 2007).

The long term course of PTSD and PTSD-related suicidality is less well characterized than the acute course of those conditions (Chatterjee et al., 2009). Survival analysis data from the NCS study demonstrated that more than one third of people with an index episode of PTSD fail to recover even after many years (Kessler et al., 1995), so the authors of that paper concluded that PTSD is often persistent. Similarly, a review of the literature by Santiago and colleagues (2013) concluded that 39% of those with PTSD have a chronic course. Spiro et al. (1994) reported that those exposed to moderate or heavy combat in WWII had 13 times greater risk of PTSD decades later. In a review of the literature, Falk and colleagues (1994) reported that older adults meet diagnostic criteria for PTSD as many as 45 years after trauma. Similarly, Dirkzwager et al. (2001) found PTSD symptoms to be present four decades after exposure to combat among older Dutch veterans of World War II. A significant association has also been reported among veterans aged 65 and older between PTSD and suicidal ideation (Durai et al., 2011). PTSD among older adults in the United States is associated with considerable psychiatric comorbidity and psychosocial dysfunction, and with mood and anxiety disorders (Pietrzak et al., 2012). The association of PTSD and suicidality is not well studied in the elderly (Marshall et al., 2001). By 2010, nearly 40% of American veterans were at least 65 years old, emphasizing the need to understand the impact of PTSD and other negative effects of military service on the mental and physical health of aging veterans (Chatterjee et al., 2009). Thus, chronic PTSD and PTSD-related suicidality are pressing current public health concerns among older veterans and non-veterans (Seal et al., 2007).

The DSM-5 diagnostic system was officially approved in 2013. The DSM-5 system for PTSD lists 20 possible symptoms and signs, grouped into four (rather than the previous three) clusters, including intrusion symptoms, avoidance, hyper-arousal, and affective symptoms (negative alterations in cognitions and mood associated with the traumatic events) (APA, 2013). The new diagnostic cluster in the proposed diagnostic system for PTSD, which was not present in DSM-IV, involves negative alteration in cognitions and mood associated with the traumatic event, as evidenced by two or more of seven listed symptoms. Thus, the diagnostic criteria for PTSD in DSM-5 have been broadened to include some depressive symptoms, (Criterion C) (Friedman et al., 2011; Elhai et al., 2012). For the first time, some depressive symptoms (which could be associated with suicidal ideations) are now part of the diagnostic criteria for PTSD in the DSM-5, though the presence of suicidal ideations is not specifically mentioned in the DSM-5 criteria for PTSD. In contrast, diagnostic criteria for PTSD in the DSM-IV did not include any mention of depressive symptoms, but instead included only symptoms associated with anxiety. Other smaller changes were also included in the DSM-5 diagnostic criteria for PTSD, though a discussion of those smaller changes is beyond the scope of this manuscript. Field trials were recently conducted to assess the reliability of selected categorical DSM-5 diagnoses, including PTSD, as obtained by two independent clinicians (Regier et al., 2013). That published manuscript reported "very good" diagnostic reliability for the DSM-5 diagnosis of PTSD in the recently conducted DSM-5 field trials. Specifically, that field trial reported a Kappa value of 0.67 for PTSD, which was higher than that for such well-established diagnoses as major depressive disorder, bipolar disorder, alcohol use disorder, and borderline personality disorder. Thus, there is recent empirical evidence from field trials which provides preliminary support for the reliability of the new diagnostic criteria for PTSD in the DSM-5, including the inclusion of depressive symptoms as one of the diagnostic criteria for PTSD. However, it is unclear whether findings concerning PTSD in younger veterans apply to chronic PTSD noted in elderly veterans (Averill & Beck, 2000). Also, the prevalence of suicidal symptoms and other depressive symptoms in veterans with PTSD, including chronic PTSD, remains unclear (Cornelius, 2013).

The study described in the current report sought to characterize the clinical picture of chronic PTSD among veterans presenting for treatment at a Veterans Affairs facility, and to assess the prevalence of suicidal ideation and suicidal behavior among those veterans. It was hypothesized that chronic PTSD noted in that sample of veterans would be characterized by prominent depressive symptoms, including prominent suicidal symptoms.

2. METHOD

2.1. Subjects

A brief pre-screen was conducted by telephone by research staff to assess whether possible participants meet eligibility criteria. Written informed consent was obtained, and potential subjects were screened for inclusion and exclusion criteria. Study subjects included male and female patients with a diagnosis of DSM -IV PTSD and/or DSM-5 PTSD. The presence of PTSD was the only inclusion criterion for participation in the study. The only exclusion criteria were an age of less than 18 years of age or the inability to read or understand study forms. The assessments for the study were conducted in a single day. The assessments were conducted at the University Drive VA over a period of two years. Assessments were completed by experienced staff persons who have had extensive training in administering the study instruments to veterans. Plans were made to discuss the clinical situation with the current treatment provider or to make appropriate clinical referrals if the results of a clinical assessment suggested that such action was needed, as per VA guidelines. A payment of $20.00 was made to participants upon completion of the study. The protocol assessment included the following instruments, all of which are commonly used, and all of which have well-documented reliability and validity:

2.2. Assessment Instruments

The Structured Clinical Interview for the DSM (SCID):

The SCID was used to determine psychiatric diagnoses (including the diagnosis of PTSD). The SCID is a semi-structured interview designed to diagnose the full range of psychiatric and substance use disorders, severity and course specifiers. The SCID was administered by experienced clinical interviewers with specialized training in SCID administration. This instrument includes a question asking about a history of trauma. The SCID has been demonstrated to have good reliability, validity, and clinical utility (First et al., 2008).

Timeline Follow-Back (TLFB): The TLFB provides a daily tabulation of drinking behavior utilizing standard drink measurement. The TLFB yields detailed information on the quantity and frequency of drinking and was used to record the past 30 days of drinking behavior. An extensive literature documents the reliability and validity of the TLFB (Sobell & Sobell, 1988). Test-retest reliabilities are typically high (0.70 - 0.94).

Beck Depression Inventory (BDI): The BDI is a widely-used well-validated 21-item participant-rated scale that measures affective, cognitive, motivational, and vegetative symptoms of depression. Items involving changes in body image, somatic preoccupation, and work difficulty were replaced. Also, sleep loss and appetite loss items were revised to assess both increases and decreases in sleep and appetite. This instrument has a high internal consistency, with Cronback alpha =0.92 (Beck et al., 1996).

Scale for Suicidal Ideation (SSI): The Scale for Suicidal Ideation (SSI) is a 19-item observer-rated scale, which assesses the current level of suicidal ideation. Three major factors are contained in the scale: 1) active suicidal desire, 2) specific plans for suicide, and 3) passive suicidal ideation (Beck et al., 1979).

Perceived Stress Scale (PSS): The PSS is a10-item self-rated instrument that was designed to measure the degree to which situations in the last month are apprised as stressful. Each of the questions is rated on a range from 0 to 4. It is a commonly used instrument. The reliability and validity of this instrument have been well established (Cohen, Kamarch, & Mermelstein, 1983).

2.3. Statistical Analysis

Descriptive statistics were calculated for all variables, including means and standard deviation for continuous variables and frequencies for categorical variables. Univariate statistical analyses were conducted using Student's t tests in the case of continuous data (e.g. BDI score) and chi-square for categorical data. All tests were two-tailed. Analyses were conducted using the SPSS, Version 15.0 (Norusis, 1992).

RESULTS

Participants in this study included 12 subjects. These subjects included 10 males (83%) and 2 females (17%); 8 (67%) were Caucasian and 4 (33%) were African-American. The mean age was 52 years, including one subject in his 70's, five subjects in their 60's, one subject in their 50's, one subject in their 40's, and four subjects in their 30's. Thus, the majority of participants were veterans of the Vietnam conflict. Marital status of participants included five who were married, 4 who were divorced, one who was separated, one who was never married, and one who was widowed. Education level of participants demonstrated three high school graduates, five who had some college, two who had a two-year college degree, one who had a four-year college degree, and one who had a graduate/professional degree. Employment status of participants showed that 3 subjects were unemployed, five were retired, four were disabled, and none were currently working.

PTSD was diagnosed in all 12 subjects, using both DSM-IV criteria and using DSM-5 criteria. All of those subjects had complained of PTSD symptoms for at least ten years, and most had complained of those symptoms for several decades, though length of PTSD symptoms had not been an inclusion requirement for participation in the study. The mean depression score on the BDI was 28.8, which was a high depression score. Scores on the BDI ranged from a low of 17 (which is still a high depression score) to a high score of 37. Half of the subjects (n =6) had a score in the range from 31 to 37, 4 subjects had BDI scores from 21 to 30, and two subjects had BDI scores in the range from 17 to 20. On question nine of the BDI, which assesses current suicidal ideations, seven subjects (n =7) reported that they currently had vague thoughts of killing themselves but would not carry them out, and five said that they did not currently have suicidal ideations. On question 20 of the SSI, which assesses the number of times that the participant has attempted suicide, four subjects (33%) reported two lifetime suicide attempts, four subjects (33%) reported one lifetime suicide attempt, and four subjects (33%) reported no lifetime suicide attempt. Thus, two-thirds of the participants had made at least one lifetime suicide attempt. However, no subject made a suicide attempt during the course of this study, and no adverse events occurred during the study. On the PSS-10, which assessed perceived stress during the last 30 days, the mean score was 25, indicating prominent stress during the most recent month, with a maximum score of 31 and a minimum score of 18. All ten of the male participants reported stress from combat exposure as a precipitant for their PTSD, while both of the female participants reported stress from sexual situations as the precipitant for their PTSD.

Depressive disorders and alcohol and substance use disorders were the most common comorbid diagnoses among participants. The most common comorbid depressive diagnoses included nine subjects with major depressive disorder and two subjects with depressive disorder, NOS. The most common substance use disorder was an alcohol use disorder, which was diagnosed in 11 subjects. However, of those 11 subjects with an alcohol use disorder, 10 had only a past diagnosis, while only one had a current diagnosis of an alcohol use disorder. Only one subject demonstrated a current non-alcohol substance use disorder, and that person demonstrated a current cannabis use disorder. However, two participants demonstrated a past diagnosis of a cannabis use disorder, one demonstrated a past diagnosis of an opioid disorder, one demonstrated a past diagnosis of a cocaine use disorder. The majority of participants reported drinking no alcohol in the most recent 30 day period, though one person reported one drink, two persons reported six drinks, one person reported 10 drinks, and one person reported 57 drinks in the most recent 30 day period.

CONCLUSION

The results of this study provide confirmation that PTSD among veterans can be chronic, and can last for decades. That finding is consistent with reports from other researchers regarding the potentially long time course of PTSD among veterans, which can last for decades (Spiro et al., 1994; Port et al., 2001; Aldwin et al., 1994). For example, Falk and colleagues (1994) found that older adults can meet diagnostic criteria for PTSD as many as 45 years after trauma, and Aldwin and colleagues (1994) found that negative consequences of combat exposure can last a lifetime. However, other researchers found somewhat different results. For example, some studies have found that PTSD symptoms are less severe the older the veterans' age (Fontana et al., 1994), while Engdahl and colleagues (1993) reported symptom stability over time for PTSD. Most of those studies did not involve longitudinal assessments, but rather involved retrospective assessment of symptoms. In one of the few longitudinal studies of trauma-related symptoms, into older adulthood, Port and colleagues found that PTSD symptoms were higher after combat exposure, decline for years, and increase in later life. Richardson et al. (2010) reported discrepant prevalence estimates of PTSD among psychiatric treatment-seeking older veterans for a variety of potential reasons. Gender differences have also been reported in regarding to reaction to trauma exposure (Creamer et al., 2008). Hyer and colleagues (1995) found that PTSD symptoms among older combat veterans are exacerbated by the problems of aging. To date, the largest and most representative longitudinal assessment of PTSD over time was conducted as part of the National Comorbidity Survey. In that study a representative national sample of 5877 persons aged 15 to 54 years in the part II subsample of the NCS. That study found that more than one third of people with an index episode of PTSD fail to recover even after many years. However, it is unclear to what extent the results from that representative national sample apply to veterans. Therefore, the trajectory of PTSD symptoms over time among veterans remains somewhat unclear.

Another finding of the current report is the prominence of suicidal symptoms and other depressive symptoms in our sample of veterans evaluated at a VA facility. That finding is consistent with the findings of a review by Krysinska and Lester (2010), who reported that PTSD is associated with an increased incidence of prior attempted suicide and prior and current suicidal ideation, even after controlling for other psychiatric disorders. In addition, Freeman and colleagues (2000) reported that higher levels of depressive symptoms are associated with increased rates of suicide attempts in persons with PTSD, and the VA study group for the current study consistently reported severe depressive symptoms, which may in part explain their high rate of suicidal symptoms. That finding raises the possibility that veterans who receive treatment for PTSD at a VA facility may generally display more prominent depressive symptoms, including suicidal symptoms, than are typically seen at non-VA settings. That possible explanation is consistent with reports that rates of depression and PTSD were considerably higher among VA outpatients than among similar patients in the private sector (Hankin et al., 1999). Alternatively, the elevated rate of suicidal behavior noted in our current sample may reflect the lifetime history of alcohol dependence that is often noted in persons with PTSD, especially veterans with PTSD (Cornelius et al., 1995). The observation that rates of lifetime suicidal behavior are high among veterans with chronic PTSD is consistent with the report of Holma and colleagues (2010), who reported that time spent depressed is likely the major factor determining overall long-term risk for suicidal behavior, while the veterans in our study group had typically displayed prominent depressive symptoms for decades.

It is noteworthy that the prevalence of current alcohol and substance use disorders was relatively low in this sample, despite the high prevalence of current depressive disorders and suicidal symptoms. Indeed, the strong majority of the alcohol and drug disorders in our sample were past (not current) disorders. Thus, over time, it appears that the veterans in the current sample demonstrated decreasing levels of drug and alcohol use, but did not demonstrate decreasing levels of depressive symptoms. That finding is consistent with reports that PTSD typically precedes substance abuse or dependence (Jacobsen and colleagues, 2001; Cornelius et al., 2010), so that the substance abuse problem could resolve and an underlying psychiatric disorder could still persist thereafter. However, it is possible that that finding reflects a selection effect rather than reflecting the natural history of PTSD among veterans, in that veterans may choose to come to the VA for treatment of their PTSD more because of their depressive symptoms rather than because of problematic alcohol and substance use.

In the current sample, a gender effect was noted in the precipitant for PTSD. Specifically, the male veterans in our sample reported combat exposure as the precipitant for their PTSD, while the female veterans in our sample reported sexual molestation as the primary precipitant for their PTSD. That finding is consistent with the findings of Kessler and colleagues (1995), who reported that the traumas most commonly associated with PTSD were combat exposure and witnessing among men and rape and sexual molestation among women, and is also consistent with the report of gender differences in trauma exposure among persons with PTSD (Creamer et al., 2008).

This study was limited by its small sample size. This study was also limited by the fact that data was only collected from veterans in the Pittsburgh VA Healthcare System, which may not be representative of veterans in other VA treatment facilities veterans across the United States. In addition, this study is limited by the fact that it did not involve longitudinal data collection, but instead collected data at only one time point. Large scale longitudinal studies are warranted to clarify the long term clinical course of PTSD among veterans, and to clarify the longitudinal clinical presentation of PTSD among various clinical and demographic subgroups (Norris et al., 2014). Also, since military-related PTSD is often a life-long disorder, systems such as the VA need to anticipate the treatment needs of veterans in their 20s-30s as possibly still requiring treatment into their 70s and 80s.

ACKNOWLEDGMENTS

This material is based upon work supported by the Department of Veterans Affairs, Veterans Health Administration, the VAPHS Office of Research and Development and the VISN 4 Mental Illness Research, Education, and Clinical Center (MIRECC, Director: D. Oslin; Pittsburgh Site Director: G. Haas), VA Pittsburgh Healthcare System. This research was also supported in part by grants from the National Institute on Alcohol Abuse and Alcoholism (R21 AA022123, R21 AA022863, R01 AA013370, R01 AA015173, and K24 AA15320) and from the National Institute on Drug

Abuse (P50 DA05605, R01 DA019142, and the NIDA Clinical Trials Network).

REFERENCES

American Psychiatric Association (2013). Diagnostic and Statistical manual of Mental Health Disorders (5th ed.). Washington, DC.

Beck, A. T., Kovacs, M. & Weissman, A. (1979). Assessment of suicidal ideation: the scale for suicidal ideation. *Journal of Consulting and Clinical Psychology*, *47*, 343-352.

Beck, A. T., Steer, R. A. & Brown, G. K. (1996). Beck Depression Inventory – Second Edition (BDI-II).

Blake, D., Keane, T. M., Wine, P. R., Mora, C., Taylor K. L. & Lyons, J. A. (1990). Prevalence of PTSD symptoms in combat veterans seeking medical treatment. *Journal of Traumatic Stress*, *3*, 15-27.

Bullman, T. A. & Kang, H. K. (1994). Posttraumatic stress disorder and the risk of traumatic deaths among Vietnam veterans. *Journal of Nervous Mental Disorders*, *182(11)*, 604-610.

Cohen, S., Kamarck, T. & Mermelstein, R. (1983). A global measure of perceived stress. *Journal of Health and Social Behavior*, *24*, 385-396.

Cornelius, J. R. (2013). Editorial regarding the new DSM-5 diagnosis of PTSD in veterans and non-veterans. *Journal of Depression & Anxiety*, *2*, 139-141.

Cornelius, J. R., Kirisci, L., Reynolds, M., Clark, D. B., Hayes, J. & Tarter, R. (2010). PTSD contributes to teen and young adult cannabis use disorders. *Addictive Behaviors*, *35*, 91-94.

Cornelius, J. R., Salloum, I. M., Mezzich, J., Cornelius, M. D., Fabrega, H., Ehler, J. G., Ulrich, R. F., Thase, M. E. & Mann, J. J. (1995). Disproportionate suicidality in patients presenting with comorbid major depression and alcoholism. *American Journal of Psychiatry*, *152*, 358-364.

Creamer, M. C. & Parslow, R. A. (2008). Trauma Exposure and Posttraumatic Stress Disorder in the Elderly: A Community Prevalence Study. *American Journal of Geriatric Psychiatry*, *16*, 853-856.

Dirkzwager, A. J. E., Bramsen, I. M. & Van Der Ploeg, H. M. (2001). The Longitudinal Course of Posttraumatic Stress Disorder Symptoms among Aging Military Veterans. *Journal of Nervous & Mental Disease*. *189*, 846-853.

Durai, U. N., Chopra, M. P., Coakley, E., Llorente, M. D., Kirchner, J. E., Cook, J. M. & Kevkoff, S. E. (2011). Exposure to trauma and posttraumatic stress disorder symptoms in older veterans attending primary care: comorbid conditions and self-rated health status. *Journal of the American Geriatric Society*, *59*, 1087-92.

Elhai, J. D., Miller, M. E., Ford J. D., Biehn, T. L., Palmieri, P. A. & Frueh, B. C. (2012). Posttraumatic stress disorder in DSM-5: Estimates of prevalence and symptom structure in a nonclinical sample of college students. *Journal of Anxiety Disorders*, *26*, 58-64.

Engdahl, B. E., Harkness, A. R., Eberly, R. E., Page, W. F. & Bielinski, J. (1993). Structural models of captivity trauma, resilience, and trauma response among former prisoners of war 20 to 40 years after release. *Social Psychiatry and Psychiatric Epidemiology*, *28*,109-115.

Falk, B., Hersen, M. & Van Hasselt, V. B. (1994). Assessment of post-traumatic stress disorder in older adults: A critical review. *Clinical Psychology Review*, *14*, 383-415.

First, M. B., Spitzer, R. L., Gibbon, M. & Williams, J. B. W. (2008). Structured Clinical Interview for DSM-IV Axis I Disorders (SCID-I). In *Handbook of Psychiatric Measures, Second Edition*, A. John Rush, Jr., Michael B. First, & Deborah Blacker, Eds. American Psychiatric Publishing, Inc., Washington, DC, 40-43.

Fontana, A. & Rosenheck, R. (1994). Traumatic war stressors and psychiatric symptoms among World War II, Korean, and Vietnam War veterans. *Psychology and Aging*, *91*, 27-33.

Freeman, T. W., Roca V. & Moore, W. M. (2000). A comparison of chronic combat-related posttraumatic stress disorder (PTSD) patients with and without a history of suicide attempt. *Journal of Nervous & Mental Disease*, *188*, 460-463.

Friedman, M. J, Resick P. A., Bryant R. A. & Brewin, C. R. (2011). Considering PTSD for DSM-5. *Depression and Anxiety*, *28*, 750-769.

Gradus, J. L., Qin, P., Lincoln, A. K., Miller, M., Lawler, H. T. S. & Lash, T. L. (2010). Posttraumatic stress disorder and completed suicide. *American Journal of Epidemiology*, *17*(6), 721-727.

Guerra, V. S., Calhoun, P. S., Mid-Atlantic Mental Illness Research, Education & Clinical Center Workgroup. (2011). Examining the relation between posttraumatic stress disorder and suicidal ideation in an OEF/OIF Veteran sample. *Journal of Anxiety Disorders*, *25*(1), 12-28.

Hankin, C. S., Spiro, A., Miller, D. R. & Kazis, L. (1999). Mental Disorders and Mental Health Treatment Among U.S. Department of Veterans

Affairs Outpatients: The Veterans Health Study. *The American Journal of Psychiatry*, *156*, 1924-1930.

Holma, K. M., Melartin, T. K., Haukka, J., Holma, I. A. K., Sokero, T. P. & Isoetsa, E. T. (2010). Incidence and Predictors of Suicide Attempts in DSM–IV Major Depressive Disorder: A Five-Year Prospective Study. *American Journal of Psychiatry*, *167*, 801-808.

Hyer, L., Summers, M. N., Braswell, L. & Boyd, S. (1995). Posttraumatic stress disorder: Silent problem among older combat veterans. *Psychotherapy: Theory, Practice and Training*, *33*, 348-364.

Institute of Medicine. (2014). Treatment for posttraumatic stress disorder in military and veteran populations: Final Assessment. Washington, D.C.: The National Academies Press.

Jacobsen L. K., Southwick, S. M. & Kosten, T. R. (2001). Substance Use Disorders in Patients With Posttraumatic Stress Disorder: A Review of the Literature. *American Journal of Psychiatry*, *158*, 1184-1190.

Jakupcak, M., Cook, J., Imel, Z., Fontana, A., Rosenheck, R. & McFall, M. (2009). Posttraumatic stress disorder as a risk factor for suicidal ideation in Iraq and Afghanistan war veterans. *Journal of Traumatic Stress*, *22*, 303-306.

Kessler, R. C., Sonnega, A., Bromet, E., Hughes, M. & Nelson, C. B. (1995). Posttraumatic Stress Disorder in the National Comorbidity Survey. *Archives of General Psychiatry*, *52*, 1048-1060.

Krysinska, K. & Lester, D. (2010). Post-Traumatic Stress Disorder and Suicide Risk: A Systematic Review. *Archives of Suicide Research*, *14*, 1-23.

LeardMann, C. A., Powell, T. M., Smith, T. C., Bell, M. R., Smith B., Boyko, E. J, Hooper, T. I., Gackstetter, G. D., Ghamsary M. & Hoge, C. W. (2013). Risk Factors Associated With Suicide in Current and Former US Military Personnel. *Journal of the American Medical Association*, *310*, 496-506.

Marshall, R. D., Olfeson, M., Hellman, F., Blanco, C., Guardino, M. & Struening, E. L. (2001). Comorbidity, impairment, and suicidality in subthreshold PTSD. *American Journal of Psychiatry*, *158*, 1467-1473.

Nepon, J., Belik, S. L., Bolton, J. & Sareen, J. (2010). The relationship between anxiety disorders and suicide attempts: findings from the National Epidemiologic Survey on Alcohol and Related Conditions. *Depression and Anxiety*, *27*, 791-798.

Nock, M. K., Stein, M. B., Heeringa, S. G., Ursano, R. J., Colpe, L. J., Fullerton, C. S., Hwang, I., Naifeh, J. A., Sampson, N. A., Schoenbaum

M., Zaslavsky, A. M. & Kessler, R. C. (2014). Prevalence and Correlates of Suicidal Behavior Among Soldiers. *JAMA Psychiatry*, *71*, 514-522.

Norris, F. H. (1992). Epidemiology of trauma: Frequency and impact of different potentially traumatic events on different demographic groups. *Journal of Consulting and Clinical Psychology*, *60*, 409-418.

Port, C. L., Engdahl, B. & Frazier P. (2001). A Longitudinal and Retrospective Study of PTSD Among Older Prisoners of War. *American Journal of Psychiatry*, *158*, 1474-1479.

Norusis, M. J. (1992). Norusis Statistical Package for the Social Sciences. McGraw-Hill, New York, USA.

Oquendo, M. A., Friend, J. M., Halberstam, B., Brodsky, B. S., Burke, A. K., Grunebaum, M. F., Malone, K. M. & Mann, J. J. (2003). Association of comorbid posttraumatic stress disorder and major depression with greater risk of suicidal behavior. *American Journal of Psychiatry*, *160*(3), 580-582.

Pietrzak, R. H., Goldstein, M. B., Malley, J. C., Rivers, A. J., Johnson, D. C. & Southwick, S. M. (2010). Risk and protective factors associated with suicidal ideation in veterans of Operations Enduring Freedom and Iraqi Freedom. *Journal of Affective Disorders*, *123*, 102-107.

Pietrzak, R. F, Goldstein, R. B., Southwick, S. M. & Grant, B. F. (2012). Psychiatric Comorbidity of Full and Partial Posttraumatic Stress Disorder Among Older Adults in the United States: Results From Wave 2 of the National Epidemiologic Survey on Alcohol and Related Conditions. *The Americal Journal of Geriatric Psychiatry*, *20*, 380-390.

Regier, D. A., Narrow, W. E., Clarke, D. E., Kramer, H. C., Kuramoto, S. J. Kuhl, E. A. & Kupfer, D. J. (2013). DSM-5 Field trials in the United States and Canada, Part II: Test-retest reliability of selected categorical diagnoses. *American Journal of Psychiatry. 170*, 71-82.

Richardson, L., Frueh, C. & Acierno, R. (2010). Prevalence Estimates of Combat-Related Post-Traumatic Stress Disorder: Critical Review. *Australian & New Zealand Journal of Psychiatry*, *44*, 4-19.

Santiago, P. N., Ursano, R. J., Gray, C. L., Pynoos, R. S., Spiegel, D., Lewis-Fernandez, R., Friedman, M. J. & Fullerton, C. S. (2013). A Systematic Review of PTSD Prevalence and Trajectories in DSM-5 Defined Trauma Exposed Populations: Intentional and Non-Intentional Traumatic Events. *PLoS ONE*, *8*, e59236.

Sayer, N. A. (2011). Response to commentary: the challenges of co-occurrence of post-deployment health problems. U.S. Department of Veterans Affairs, Health Services Research and Development Service,

Washington, DC, from http://www.hsrd. research.va.gov/publications/forum/may11/may112.cfm.

Schoenbaum, M., Kessler, R. C., Gilman, S. E., Colpe L. J., Heeringa, S. G., Stein, M. B., Ursano, R. J. & Cox, K. L. (2014). Predictors of Suicide and Accident Death in the Army Study to Assess Risk and Resilience in Servicemembers (Army STARRS): Results from the Army Study to Assess Risk and Resilience in Servicemembers (Army STARRS). *JAMA Psychiatry*, *71*, 493-503.

Seal, K. H., Bertenthal, D., Miner, C. R., Sen, R., & Marmar, C. (2007). Bringing the war back home: Mental health disorders among 103,788 US veterans returning from Iraq and Afghanistan seen at Department of Veterans Affairs facilities. *Archives of Internal Medicine*, *12*, 476-482.

Sobell, L. C., Sobell, M. B., Leo, G. I., Cancilla, A. (1988). Reliability of a timeline method: assessing normal drinkers' reports of recent drinking and a comparative evaluation across several populations. *British Journal of Addiction*, *83*(4), 393-402.

Spiro, A., Schnurr, P. P. & Aldwin, C. M. (1994). Combat-related posttraumatic stress disorder symptoms in older men. *Psychology and Aging*, *9*, 17-26.

In: Suicidal Ideation
Editor: Bradley Weaver
ISBN: 978-1-63483-092-8

Chapter 3

GENETICS AND BIOINFORMATICS STUDY OF ANTIDEPRESSANT DRUGS, RECENT ADVANCEMENTS AND FUTURE TRENDS

Da-Yong Lu[1,*], Ting-Ren Lu[2], Peng-Peng Zhu[3] and Jin-Yu Che[1]

[1]Shanghai University, Shanghai, PR China
[2]College of Science, Shanghai University, Shanghai, PR China
[3]Cellular Neurology Unit, NINDS, National Institute of Health, US

ABSTRACT

Despite widely clinical applications, during the early 1990s, emergence the episodes of patients' suicide receiving antidepressants, especially in children was reported. As for 2004, the US and European regulatory authority began implementing verification programs to assess the influence on suicidal behavior from the use of antidepressants. With the increasing number of cases reported, several newly developed antidepressants are facing withdrawn from the market. Although the underlying mechanisms of action for drugs-induced suicide remained unclear, researches focusing on revealing the relationship between efficacy and toxicities of antidepressants have been initiated in China and US. To counteract this situation, genetic study of anti-depressant induced

* Corresponding author: Dr Da-Yong Lu, School of Life Sciences, Shanghai University, Shanghai 200444, PR China, ludayong@sh163.net; ludayong@shu.edu.cn.

suicidal behaviors and other toxicity episode has been started. More than one hundred research papers, perspectives and reviews have been published. This chapter will depict the recent advances of these researches and offers the possible initiations for future investigations

Keywords: Human genome, drug risk, drug response, neural toxicity, genetics, medicinal chemistry, next generation sequencing

INTRODUCTION

Human depression epidemics are growing worldwide in the last decade, possibly due to economic crisis in most countries. Depression is known as one of the most common psychiatric illnesses with an estimated prevalence of 15-20% within the general population [Lucas, 2008, Menchetti et al., 2010, Menchetti, et al., 2014]. Since large proportion of human beings suffers emotional depression in highly competitive modern society, negative impacts on healthy progresses of society have been reluctantly seen. With the development of a series of antidepressants, certain amount of depressed persons improves their depressive emotions by given antidepressants [Lucas, 2008, Menchetti et al., 2010, Menchetti, et al., 2014]. However, these types of antidepressant therapies like a double-edged sword that has both strengths and weaknesses. As early as 1990, antidepressants were reported to induce suicidal events in clinical trials [Teicher et al., 1990]. In order to overcome these obstacles of antidepressant therapies, some good examples and paradigms have been speculated and systematically investigated over the past decade. Excellent future miracles can be foreseeable.

SUICIDAL IDEATION/ATTEMPT AND ANTIDEPRESSANT TREATMENTS

Despite widely utilizations of antidepressants, some depressed people who seek the help of therapeutic interventions exhibit undesired toxicities even patients' suicidal episodes, especially in children and teenagers [Brent et al., 2010, Lu et al., 2007, Lu and Lu, 2011, Rubino et al., 2007, Tsai, 2005]. By entering into this millennium, the US and European regulatory authorities began implementing verification programs to assess the influence on suicidal behavior from the use of antidepressants such as selective serotonin reuptake inhibitors (SSRIs), drug's safety in patients has renewed as a criteria indispensable for approving or withdrawing drugs [Check, 2004, Holden, 2004]. The hustling and bustling among antidepressant manufacturer retrospective effort escalated and actions by drug regulatory authority tightened. Just following this dilemma, it is hypothesized that human's genetic makeup might affect the episodes of suicidal ideations in patients receiving antidepressants [Lu et al., 2007]. Parallel to our suggestions, the relationship between suicidal ideation by different types of antidepressants and human single nucleotide polymorphisms (SNPs) has been preliminary built [Brent, et al., 2010, Kuo, et al., 2013, Lu et al., 2012b, Lu et al., 2013, Lu et al., 2014a]. Since the causations of antidepressant-induced undesired events might be multi-factorials, scientific investigations of each biological, toxicological and environmental factors interrelated with patient suicidal ideation/attempt, self-injure, self-harm etc are indispensable. These possibilities are outlined in this chapter.

Antidepressant Therapy PG and Bioinformatics

As aforementioned, PG technology detects genes of many biological or pharmacological interests and is mainly divided into two general categories—predicting risks and response by drug-related pathways and drug concentrations of absorption, distribution, metabolism and excretion (ADME) by SNPs of human drug metabolic enzymes or drug transporting molecules or others. Approximately 300 metabolic enzymes have been found in human bodies. Many antidepressant drugs are metabolized through CYP2D6. Among these PG (pharmacogenetics) or bioinformatics studies, only detections of drugs and their metabolites in human blood and bodies by modern chromatography [Kuo et al., 2013] can parallel with metabolic enzyme (SNPs) and achieve useful clinical outcomes. The genetic polymorphism changes of metabolic enzymes decrease or increase the blood concentrations of antidepressants by different active rates of drug ADME, which decide main parts of drug toxicities in human bodies. The therapeutic (risks) or efficacy predictions of different types of antidepressants by SNPs of ADME outcomes, such as fatigue and vomiting etc., are exemplified in the advent of several hospital routines. The studies of drug-toxic or drug-efficacy molecules are great therapeutic significances. A strong relationship exists between blood concentration, therapeutic side effects or efficacies of many psychiatric drugs.

According to clinical circumstances, drug-toxic or drug-targeted molecules are proposed to be different mechanisms of action. Neural molecules or receptors have been proposed to be major gene encoding for both the suicidal ideations occurrence (risk) and therapeutic responses and outcomes (antidepressant drug efficacies) [Kuo et al., 2013, Lu et al., 2013, Lu et al., 2014a].

Despite the long-term accumulations of genetic studies and clinical data of neural toxicity of drugs, currently antidepressant PG or bioinformatics play minor roles in establishing safety of an investigational drug. Safety is still largely determined through empirical observation of large cohorts of patients in randomized clinical trials. A strong relationship exists between blood concentration, therapeutic efficacies and side effects for monitoring psychiatric drug treatments. Some new problems are emerged thereby creating new insights into antidepressant PG and bioinformatics studies and applications. Since the efficacies and risks of antidepressant drugs might be caused by same pathways, it is proposed that they can be detected in the same route (kill two birds by only one stone) [Lu et al., 2014a]. This untested strategy is presently different from most other types of diseases and therapeutic modes. Before pursuing this hypothesis, formal investigative routes and scientific foresights have to be designed first.

The best gene candidates for antidepressant therapy predictions are unclear now. Genetic panels affecting both drug-active and drug-toxic genes (molecules) in the same times might be priority for in-depth scientific investigations and therapeutic significances.

Methodologies Presently Available

Optogenetics—many genes of neural molecules or receptors have been incorporated with light-sequence and systematic studies in cells and animals.

GEM—genetic engineering mice have been applied for studying the mechanisms of action or toxicities of antidepressants.

PG—genetic determinations of human metabolic enzymes, such as CYP2D6 for predictions of therapeutic efficacies and toxicities, separately or combine.

Drug-active or drug-toxic genes (SNPs)—clinical detections of drug-related molecules and pathways.

Genome-wide association studies (GWAS) of antidepressants.

New genetic or molecular studies.

Table 1. Roadmap of Antidepressant Studies

Research System	Related Pathways and Mechanisms of Action
Mathematics	Different equation developments and calculations
Physics	Structure and configurations of antidepressants Quantum physics calculation Environmental factors
Chemistry	Medicinal chemistry for different types of antidepressants Quantum chemistry Modern chromatography
Genetic or genomic	Genome wide associate study Pharmacogenetics or pharmacogenomics PCR or other general biological systems Non-encoding DNA RNA-editing Next generation sequencing Genetic-engineering mice (GEM)
Molecular information	Bioinformatics Immune-related assays (antibody) Micro-RNA HPLC-MS-MS
In vitro models	Different cell types Biomarker studies Optogenetics or other modern technologies RNA-editing
In vivo models	Response and toxicity evaluations in animals Modern chromatography Bioinformatics testing and identifications GEM Next-generation sequencing
Humans	Genome-wide associate study Pharmacogenomics Next-generation sequencing Different bioinformatics detecting, identifications and verifications Statistical analysis Meta-analysis Modern chromatography and other analytical instruments PCR and other modern biological means Personalized therapy

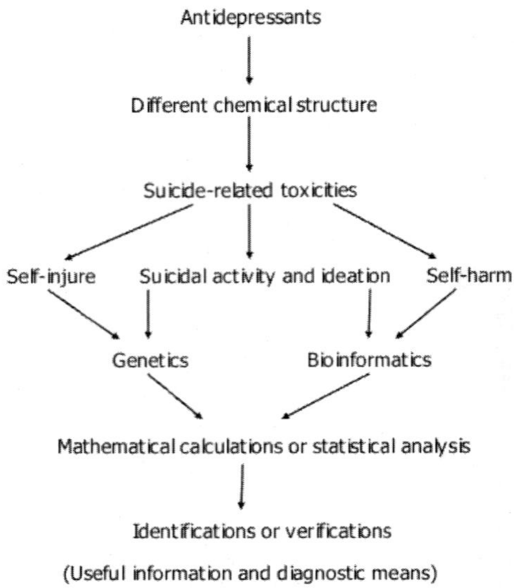

Figure 1. Possible schemes for toxicology of antidepressant treatment studies.

DISCUSSIONS AND FUTURE TRENDS

Personalized Therapy

In order to decrease or even prevent many unnecessary toxicities and maximum treatment efficacies by antidepressants in clinics, personalized therapy (PT) of antidepressant treatments will be future trends [Lu et al., 2014a]. This seems to be true in all medical disciplines or PT [Lu et al., 2014b]. Despite the popularity of PT worldwide, antidepressant therapeutics by PT are not overwhelmed. Yet their future applications and successes are highly expected. It is suggested that antidepressant treatment PT can be mandatory in developed countries for its cost-effective protocols and higher therapeutic efficacies than ever before.

Genome-Wide Association Study (GWAS) of Antidepressant Therapy

GWAS study of biomedical problems is always the priority for modern therapeutic advancements. Predicting neural toxicity (risks) and responses of antidepressants between normal human beings and depressed patients by GWAS identifies more than ten genetic allele differences between normal and antidepressant susceptible humans [Garriock et al., 2010, Laja et al., 2009, Menke et al., 2012, Uher et al., 2010]. Since only half of these alleles are statistical significance now, it may be explained as being affected by other genetic or environmental factors or shortages of human genomic sample sizes [Lu et al., 2014a]. It is the time for finding workable roadmap to transform antidepressant therapy from experimental investigations into clinical paradigms (from bench to the bedside). For GWAS, next generation sequencing (NGS) techniques (increase the speed of genome sequencing 15,000-50,000 times) and dramatically reduce the cost of genome sequencing (less than ten thousand US dollar for one genome) [Collins, 2010, Lander, 2011, Venter, 2010] can speed up our understanding the relationship between human genetics and risk issue of antidepressant therapy. Since human suicide is a rare symptom of human beings (10/100,000), the genetic or genomic study of this characteristic needs a great deal of human population data (at lease 10, 000 to 50,000 genetic pools). Otherwise, the outcomes of experimental or clinical data studies and underlying mechanisms of action revelations by drugs may be undermined. In order to meet such requirements of so many varieties of human genomic information, it needs huge amount of money/personnel or world-wide cooperation. It is very difficult to study it by a single hospital or lab at present stage. Only great technical achievements or world-wide cooperation can solve this problem.

Finding More Biological Information from Non-Encoding DNA Sequencing Regions

It has been widely accepted that protein-encoding regions are accounted for just 1.5% of the human genome and transcription-controlling sites DNA are also in small part of human genomes. Could the rest of our genomes (largely repeated short DNA) really just be unimportant, or even regarded as junks [Pennisi, 2010]? Are the repetitive "junk" DNA and epigenetic systems related with drug-induced neural toxicity or risks of antidepressants? Whether the copy numbers or different sequences of repetitive DNA vary in different drug sensitive persons? These open questions proposed for a couple of years ago need to be convincingly answered and scientifically proved in future [Lu et al., 2013, Lu et al., 2014a]. By NGS techniques, more useful information relating to these relationships may be found and accumulated. It may evaluate and fuel with the systematic studies of many new ideas and arguments and finally help to transform these new initiatives into practical ones with much less costs.

ENVIRONMENTAL FACTORS

Environmental factors play pivotal roles in suicidal occurrence because suicidal rates up and down every one to two decades. If only genetic factor can affect human depressive emotions or suicide, the suicidal rates will be stable all the times. But it will not detain our efforts for finding the mystery between human genetics and suicidal occurrences. Since many environmental factors greatly affect the rate of suicidal incidence, self-harm or self-injure, it exhibits much difficulty for genetic or bioinformatics studies of antidepressant responses and toxicities. These environmental factors can be depression, alcohol- or drug-related problems, poverty, social status, debts, job-loss (unemployment) and divorce etc., [Duffy, 2009, Kapur & Gask, 2009]. Since many environmental factors are potential threats to statistical analysis of valuable clinical data, may we suggest move out many biased patients in clinical antidepressant evaluations and verifications?

Previously, we gave an equation of drug toxicities affected by following factors [Lu & Lu, 2011]

$$P_{toxicity} = P_{chemical} + P_{genetic} + P_{environment}$$

In future, more experimental or clinical data should be used to calculate different possibilities of toxicities of antidepressant treatments.

Technical Selections and Clinical Outcomes of Antidepressant Studies

Biological methods for experimental and clinical researches are huge numbers and can be divided into different categories and be used in different circumstances (Table 1). Nevertheless, no single biological method is suitable for all clinical occasions and circumstances. Utilizations of avant-garde methodologies and instruments need mounting money and human resources. Yet these efforts can increase our understanding of these matters and clinically more cautious upon these types of evidence for intending antidepressant therapeutics.

Modern biological, pharmacological and toxicological techniques have been developed greatly for antidepressant treatments, such as optogenetic studies [Lu et al., 2012b, Lu et al., 2013, Zhao et al., 2013] or genetic engineering mice (GEM) [Youngtrom & Strowbridge, 2012] and other new technologies and patents [Lu et al., 2014a], are commonly used to assess many opening hypotheses [Lu et al., 2007] and finally predict antidepressant therapy PG or bioinformatics. Other revolutionary clinical diagnostic and therapeutic systems are underway. The techniques of optogenetic and GEM are new endeavors that can be used to study the functions and dysfunctions of specific genes in living bodies. Nonetheless, these newly discovered technologies can be a large flood in futuristic antidepressant therapy studies. Only then, many longstanding controversies can be resolved. As previously suggested, all drugs with hepato-toxicity will be removal from markets [Shah, 2006]. According to Shah, hepato-toxicities of drugs are rarely rescued by different types of personalized therapy (PT) researches. For mechanisms of action of suicidal episode by antidepressant drug therapies is still a mystery and hot topic for modern PT studies and applications in clinics. Since almost every drug was withdrawn from market for PT hepato-toxicities in humans, further experimental work by using GEM with human hepatic gene engineered mice might be able to answer questions like that. So in future, a lot of intrinsic related things behind the scenery can be discovered by increasing worldwide cooperative efforts and new generations of technologies and lab equipments. These researches will make great impacts on antidepressant therapies not only on medicinal chemistry inquisitions, but also on pharmacology and toxicology disciplines. Only more sophisticated evaluation or identification methods must be renovated for the purposes of analyzing multi-variant information in antidepressant therapies.

Borrow Lesson from Similar Study

Borrow lessons from similar study can promote the PG or bioinformatics studies of antidepressant agents having neural toxicities, such as antimicrobial-induced mania [Abouesh et al., 2002, Baranowski, 2010, Fidan & Fidan, 2009, Lu et al., 2012b, Tome & Filipe, 2011] or antimicrobial-induced hearing loss and so on [Lu et al., 2010, Lu et al., 2014a]. Previously, though a line of clinical evidence of antimicrobial-induced mania has been reviewed, no widely acceptable answer has been given. Genetic study on the relationship between drug-induced toxicity and human genetic variation is lacking due to rare incidence of neural toxicities in patients and normal persons, which makes them unsuited for genetic study. But it can be well explained by genetic theory. We believe this type of study could not do in vain. By discovering genetic alleles of antibiotics-induced persons, we can learn a lot of new information of biomedical importance and clinical significances. It might be an indispensable part of anti-microbial agent development. It is a meaningful job but sample limiting. Only world-wide cooperation can solve this problem. A lot of drug-induced ototoxicities by aminoglycoside treatments is caused by genetic polymorphisms—SNP (single nucleotide polymorphism) in some mitochondrial genes of patients [Lu et al., 2010]. In future, treatment insurance might be considered in the study and clinical applications of different types of antidepressant therapies.

Finally, possible future avenues and roadmap for antidepressant therapy PG or bioinformatics systems are summarized as followings.

Summary

I: Previous Hypotheses and Present Available Therapeutic Means

- Judgments and identifications of the relationships between environmental factors and suicidal incidence in different human populations have been found.
- Integration of drug toxic (suicidal ideations)—disease progression (patients' depression)-score index into one system and make them available for experimental or clinical therapeutic studies and applications
- GWAS of antidepressant therapy has been accumulated.
- Many new techniques, such as PG or bioinformatics have been used in many ways.

II: New Ideas and Technologies

- Support and promote novel ideas and techniques that can help and fuel the assessments and evaluating new generation of hypotheses and create more suitable therapeutic means.
- Create and finding more effective patents that help implementing antidepressant treatment and risk/response evaluating and prediction systems in future.
- Investigations of neural related genes, biological molecules and their functions (genotypic or phenotypic information) by new techniques such as opto-genetics study or genetic engineering mice (GEM) and so on.
- Drafting more human genomes (large pools or sizes of individuals and populations) and finding the relationship between different genetics, bioinformatics and phenotype (risk/response) by different types of antidepressant drugs with next-generation of sequencing (NGS) technology.
- Scientifically investigating on the relationship between pathogenesis and therapeutics of antidepressant treatments by medicinal chemistry or personalized therapies.

III: Future Trends

- Genetic or genomic study of repeated DNA in human genomes that may make difference in new drug discoveries, developments and clinical applications.
- Collect data of relationship between genetics, molecular, chemical and environmental factors and drug (antidepressant) efficacies and neural toxicities.
- Genome-wide association study (GWAS) of more depressed patients and normal persons of different pathogenic conditions, ethnic groups/races, family inheritable diseases, genders or ages. For these work, worldwide cooperation and scientific investigations among different disciplinary scientists are urgently needed.
- Invitation of more mathematics or physics major students and scholars to join hands with biomedical major students and scientists in genomic sequencing, data analysis and clinical therapeutic efficacies and toxicities predictions.

- Systems biology, mathematics and calculating models/systems investigations for in-depth understanding the intrinsic relationship between diagnosis and therapies.
- Accumulating rare family inherence disease cases of human genomes as many as possible and GWAS study of rare occurred inherent diseases should be joined and relationship between chemical, genetic or environmental factors must be found and promoted.
- Budget control all scientific investigations and clinical depressive disordered patients' therapies so that these researches can help depressed people as many as possible.
- Further investigations on etiological or pathological mechanisms of human suicide or self-harm and so on.
- Learn the lesson from beyond, such as the study of anti-microbial.

Conclusion Remarks

In future, more attentions should be paid on different possibilities of drug-induced neural toxicities. We look forward more scientific work that promotes personalize antidepressant therapies in hospital routine and protocols. Presently, many questions and controversies need to be resolved. Some unexpected scientific discoveries and technical advancements (such as NGS etc) might lead us into new horizons and enough effective diagnostic and therapeutic means will be renovated. We only wish this perspective may speed up these therapeutic studied and applications greatly.

Acknowledgments

This work was funded by Shanghai Science and Technology Foundation of High Educations 97A49

References

Abouesh, et al. (2002). Antimicrobial-induced mania (antibiomania): a review of spontaneous reports. *J Clin Psychopharmacol.*, *22* (1), 71-81.

Baranowski, W. J. (2010). Clarithromycin-induced hypomania in a child—a case report. *Acta Psychiatr Scand, 122* (3), 267-268.

Brent, D., et al. (2010). Pharmacogenomics of suicidal events. *Pharmacogenomics. 11*(6), 793-807.

Check, E. (2004). Drug suicide risks prompt call for FDA action. *Nature, 427*(6974), 474.

Collins, F. (2010). Has the revolution arrived. *Nature, 464* (7289), 674-675.

Duffy, D. (2009). Self-injury. *Psychiatry, 8*(7), 237-240.

Fidan, T. & Fidan, V. (2009). Clarithromycin-induced mania in a child. *Int J Clinical Pharmacol Therapeutics. 47* (6), 402-404.

Garriock, et al. (2010). A genome wide association study of citalopram response in major depressive disorder. *Biol Psychiatry. 67* (2), 133-138.

Holden, C. (2004). FDA weighs suicide risk in children on antidepressants. *Science*, 2004, *303* (5659), 745.

Kapur, N. & Gask, L. (2009). Introduction to suicide and self-harm. *Psychiatry, 8*(7), 233-236.

Kuo, et al. (2013). CYP1A2 genetic polymorphisms are associated with early antidepressant escitalopram metabolism and adverse reactions. *Pharmacogenomics. 14*(10), 1191-1201.

Laje, et al. (2009). Genome-wide association study of suicidal ideation emerging during citalopram treatment of depressed outpatients. *Pharmacogenet Genomics. 19* (9), 666-674.

Lander, E. S. (2011). Initial impact of the sequencing of the human genome. *Nature, 470* (7333), 187-197.

Lu, D. Y., et al. (2007). May genetic factors play a role in the risk of antidepressant-induced suicide. *Med Hypotheses. 69* (6), 1380-2381.

Lu, D. Y., et al. (2010). Undesired neural side-effects of a drug, a chemical and genetic interrelated problem. *Central Nervous System Agent Medicinal Chemistry. 10*(2), 108-112.

Lu, D. Y. & Lu, T. R. (2011). Importance of genomic studies for drug withdrawal with mental illness. *Drug Therapy Studies, 1*(1), e11.

Lu, D. Y., et al. (2012a). The hypotheses for the pathogeny of drug-induced mania and suicide. *Adv Pharmacoepidemiol Drug Safety. 1* (5). e114.

Lu, D. Y., et al. (2012b). Genetics in neural toxicities of drugs. *Central Nervous System Agent Medicinal Chemistry, 12* (4), 250-253.

Lu, D. Y., et al. (2013). Pharmacogenetics in neural toxicities of drugs. *Pharmacogenomics, 14* (10), 1129-1131.

Lu, D. Y., et al. (2014a). Genetics and bioinformatics studies of antidepressant drug therapeutic efficacies and toxicities, a current overview. *Recent Pat CNS Drug Discov. 9*(3), 193-199.

Lu D. Y. (2014b). Personalized cancer chemotherapy, an effective way for enhancing outcomes in clinics. Woodhead Publishing & Elsevier, UK.

Lucas, G. (2008). Fast-acting antidepressants: are we nearly there. *Expert Rev Neurotherapeutics. 8*(1), 1-3.

Menchetti, M., et al. (2010). Depression in primary care: Interpersonal counseling *vs* selective serotonin reuptake inhibitors. The DEPICS study. A multicenter randomized controlled trial. Rationale and design. *BMC Psychiatry. 10*, 97.

Menchetti, M., et al. (2014). Moderators of remission with interpersonal counseling or drug treatment in primary care patients with depression: randomized controlled trial. *Br J Psychiatry, 204* (2), 144-150.

Menke, et al. (2012). Genome-wide association study of antidepressant treatment-emergent suicidal ideation. *Neuropsychopharmacology, 37*(3), 797-807.

Menke, et al. (2012). Polymorphisms within the metabotropic glutamate receptor 1 gene are associated with depression phenotypes. *Psychneuroendocrinology, 37*(4), 565-575.

Pennisi, E. (2010). Shining a light on the genome's 'dark matter.' *Science, 330* (6011), 1614.

Rubino, A., et al. (2007). Risk of suicide during treatment with venlafaxine, citalopram, fluoxetine, and dothiepin: retrospective cohort study. *BMJ, 334*(7587), 242-247.

Shah, R. R. (2006). Can pharmacogenetics help rescue drugs withdrawn from the market? *Pharmacogenomics, 7* (6), 889-908.

Teicher, M. H., et al. (1990). Emergence of intense suicidal preoccupation during fluoxetine treatment. *Am J Psychiatry. 147*(2), 207-10.

Tome, A. M. & Filipe, A. (2011). Quinolones: review of psychiatric and neurological adverse reaction. *Drug Safety, 34*(6), 465-488.

Tsai, S. J. (2005). Possible involvement of the BDNF-dependent pathway in the treatment-emergent suicidality or decreased response to antidepressants. *Med Hypotheses, 65* (5), 942-946.

Uher, et al. (2010). Genome-wide pharmacogenetics of antidepressant response in the GENDEP project. *Am J Psychiatry. 167* (5), 555-564.

Venter, J. C. (2010). Multiple personal genomes await. *Nature, 464* (7289), 676-677.

Youngtrom, I. A. & Strowbridge, B. W. (2012). Visual landmarks facilitate rodent, spatial navigation in virtual reality environment. Learn Mem, 2012, *9* (3), 84-90.

Zhao, Y., et al. (2013). Human dopamine transporter gene: differential regulation of 18-kb haplotypes. *Pharmacogenomics*, *14*(12), 1481-1494.

In: Suicidal Ideation
Editor: Bradley Weaver
ISBN: 978-1-63483-092-8

Chapter 4

THE HYPOTHESES FOR THE PATHOGENS OF ANTIMICROBIAL-INDUCED MANIA AND SUICIDE

Da-Yong Lu[1,*], Ting-Ren Lu[2], Peng-Peng Zhu[3] and Hong-Ying Wu[2]

[1]School of Life Sciences, Shanghai University, Shanghai, PR China
[2]College of Science, Shanghai University, Shanghai, PR China
[3]Cellular Neurology Unit, NINDS, National Institute of Health, US

ABSTRACT

In 2002, Abouesh's reviewed the phenomenon of rarely occurrences of spontaneous antimicrobial-induced mania in western world. Lately, increasing cases and reports of clinical evidence have supported this issue again and again, especially in kids and teenagers. Yet the mechanisms of action for the relationship of this phenomenon behind the scenario are still missing. After carefully analyzing references and reports, we have found that it is very similar with our previous suggests the relationship between patient suicide by antidepressant treatments and human genetic factors. Thus we speculate the some drug-induced toxicological characters vs the therapeutic efficacies and mechanisms of action of

[*] Corresponding author: Dr Da-Yong Lu ludayong@sh163.net, ludayong@shu.edu.cn.

different types of drugs by genetics and bioinformatics considerations and investigations. Further explanations from many newly published data and references are enlisted and separately analyzed. Comparisons and mechanistic investigation borrowed from the work of other categories of drugs and neural toxicity types are also highlighted in this chapter.

Keywords: Antibiotics, antidepressant, mania, suicide, genetics, bioinformatics, toxicity, psychiatry

INTRODUCTION

As for 2004, the US and European regulatory agencies began implementing verification programs to assess the influence on suicidal behavior from the use of antidepressants such as selective serotonin reuptake inhibitors (SSRIs) [Check 2004, Holden 2004]. With the increasing number of cases reported, several newly developed antidepressants were withdrawn from the market despite unknown mechanisms of action behind this scenario. It has been posited that some antidepressants may induce anxiety or mania, and thus their use should be cautious. On the other hand, since it is possible that the side effects associated with use of these drugs may be individuals rather than all population, we hypothesized that genetic factor might account for drug-induced suicidal behavior [Lu et al., 2007]. Later, more and more clinical data correspond with our hypothesis [Brent et al. 2010, Lu et al., 2012b].

THE ORIGINATIONS OF ANTI-MICROBIAL-INDUCED MANIA STUDY

In 2002, Abouesh's reviewed [Abouesh et al., 2010] the phenomenon of rarely occurrences of spontaneous antimicrobial-induced mania in western world. Soon after, more and more clinical evidence of this phenomenon has repeated and reported world-wide [Baranowski, 2010, Fidan & Fidan, 2009, Lu et al., 2012a, Tome & Filipe, 2011]. Yet their mechanisms of action are still missing. After perusal of these lines of clinical data, we have found that it is very similar with our previous hypothesis for antidepressant [Lu et al.,

2012b]. Thus a hypothesis relating mechanisms of action for drug-induced toxicology is further explained [Lu et al., 2012a].

HYPOTHESES OF THE PATHOGENY OF ANTIMICROBIAL OR ANTIDEPRESSANT-INDUCED MANIA AND SUICIDE

In particular, it is feasible that specific genetic polymorphisms affecting the serotonin-related pathways and systems that its function is associated with body anxiety, mania, self-injure and suicidal etc. Similarly, genetic mutations, copying, deleting, translocation or polymorphisms may exert an influence on the expression of a number of drug-metabolizing enzymes, such as the cytochrome P-450 enzymes that are responsible for the biotransformation of most antidepressants. Polymorphisms of genes controlling these enzymes could also be associated with the presence of various kinds of side effects, including violence and self-harm [Ingelman-Sundberg, 2005, Taylor and Stein, 2006]. Future pharmacogenomics and whole-genome genetic association studies [Garriock et al., 2010, Laje et al., 2009, Lu et al., 2014, Menke et al., 2012(a), Menke et al., 2012(b)] especially on antimicrobial-induced mania patients, are needed to confirm previous hypothesis and establish good therapeutic paradigms.

In considerations of its clinical observations and patients' abnormal brain episodes, we herein add two more suggestions; (i) rapid recovery mechanisms of action by genetic changes of neural genetic or molecular functions by antimicrobial treatments; Antimicrobials may trigger the escalated productions of some mania-related factors such as GABA or prostaglandins by over-burdened central nerve cells; (ii) if relative concentrations of drugs in blood is important for the symptoms of mania. Genetic mutations, polymorphisms, copying, deleting or translocations of genes of drug metabolizing enzymes, such as cytochrome P450 may play more decisive roles than polymorphisms of mental functioning molecules because such actions will in general elicit complicated genetic consequences and symptoms and last longer; These hypotheses could be easily verified by further clinical blood drug concentration tests by modern chromatography in patients or possible drug-related mental diseases or side-effects are studied.

Madness is not the same thing as suicide episode. But we propose that there is positive relationship between them as they are all in states of neural pathogenesis and out of minds. In this initial stage of scientific investigations for antimicrobial applications, more neural toxicities alike to madness should be subjected into genetic comparisons and statistic analysis across large human populations. Psychiatry score systems and environmental factors may be proposed to a conventional way for identifying key elements that affect the neural toxicities by antimicrobial treatments.

Current Achievements

- The discovery of antimicrobials-induced mania [Abouesh et al., 2002, Baranowski, 2010, Fidan & Fidan, 2009, Tome & Filipe, 2011] and so on.
- The discovery of antimicrobial-induced deafness [Lu et al., 2010] and so on.
- Genetic assessments of drug-induced ototoxicities [Li et al., 2005, Lu et al., 2010, Scrimshaw et al., 1999, Xie et al., 1997, Xing et al., 2006] and so on.
- Medicinal chemistry/clinical mania episode relationship has been studied worldwide [Tome & Filipe, 2011].
- New proposals and strategies for neural toxicities of antimicrobials [Lu et al., 2012].

Methodologies and Investigative Proposals

Since the antimicrobials-induced neural toxicities are a rare symptom of human beings, the genetic or genomic study of this characteristic needs a great deal of human population data (at lease 10, 000 to 50,000 genetic pools). Otherwise, the outcomes of experimental or clinical data studies and underlying mechanisms of action revelations by drugs may be undermined. In order to meet such requirements of so many varieties of human genomic information, it needs huge amount of money/personnel or world-wide cooperation. It is very difficult to study it by a single hospital or lab at present stage. The proposed schemes of further studies are given in Figure 1. (Figure 1)

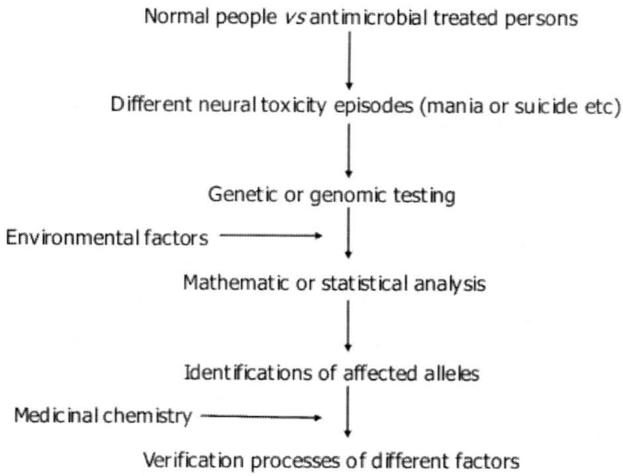

Figure 1. The proposed schemes of further genetic or genomic studies of antimicrobial treatments.

CURRENT TECHNICAL SELECTIONS FOR MANIA OR SUICIDAL STUDY

Basic biological, pharmacological and toxicological information changes determined by modern techniques such as optogenetic studies [Li et al., 2005, Lu et al., 2010, Scrimshaw et al., 1999, Xie et al., 1997, Xing et al., 2006] or genetic engineering mice (GEM) [Youngtrom IA and Strowbridge BW, 2012] and other new technologies and patents [Lu et al., 2013, Lu et al., 2014] after antimicrobial or antidepressant treatments, are commonly used to assess or verify many opening hypotheses and promote systematic scientific studies, and finally update antimicrobial or antidepressant therapies in other clinical diagnostic and therapeutic routines in modern hospitals. The techniques of optogenetic and GEM are new endeavors that can be used to study the functions and dysfunctions of specific genes in living bodies. Nonetheless, these newly discovered technologies can be a large flood in futuristic antidepressant therapy studies. Only then, many longstanding controversies can be resolved. As previously suggested, all drugs with hepato-toxicity will be removal from markets [Shah, 2006]. According to Shah, hepato-toxicities of drugs are rarely rescued by different types of personalized therapy (PT) researches. For mechanisms of action of suicidal episode by antidepressant drug therapies is still a mystery and hot topic for modern PT studies and applications in clinics. Since almost every drug was withdrawn from market for PT hepato-toxicities in humans, further experimental work by using GEM with human hepatic gene engineered mice might be able to answer questions like that. So in future, a lot of intrinsic related things behind the scenery can be discovered by increasing worldwide cooperative efforts and new generations of technologies and lab equipments. These researches will make great impacts on antidepressant therapies not only on medicinal chemistry inquisitions, but also on pharmacology and toxicology disciplines. Only more sophisticated evaluation or identification methods must be renovated for the purposes of analyzing multi-variant information in antidepressant therapies.

Investigations of neural related genes, biological molecules and their functions by new techniques such as opto-genetics study or genetic engineering mice (GEM) and so on.

Systems biology, mathematics and calculating models/systems investigations for in-depth understanding the intrinsic relationship between diagnosis and therapeutics.

Drafting more human genomes (large sizes of individuals and populations) and finding the relationship between different genetics or bioinformatics and risk/response criteria.

Build the relationship between genetics, molecular, chemical and environmental factors and drug (antimicrobials) efficacies and neural toxicities.

Genome-wide association study (GWAS) of more depressed patients and normal persons of different pathogenic conditions or environmental factors, ethnic groups/races, family inheritable diseases, genders or ages.

Invitation of more mathematics or physics major students and scholars to join hands with biomedical major students and scientists in human genomic sequencing, data analysis and clinical therapeutic efficacies and toxicities predictions [Lu et al., 2014].

Invitation of Genome-Wide Association Study (GWAS) for Both Antidepressant and Antimicrobial Therapies

Invitation of genome-wide association study (GWAS) for both antidepressant and antimicrobials therapies might lead to the final solutions for predicting neural toxicity (risks) and responses between antidepressants and antimicrobials to normal human beings and relevant patients and finally understanding all information of antimicrobials risks and responses in clinical trials. By taking GWAS, more than ten genetic allele difference between normal and antidepressant susceptible humans have been found [Garriock et al., 2010, Laje et al., 2009, Menke et al., 2012(a), Menke et al., 2012(b)]. Further work is needed for helping us to resolve this matter and find more genetic alleles of clinical significance from large sized human genome populations by different types of drugs such as antimicrobials and antidepressants and so on. It is a workable avenue for transformations of antidepressant therapy from experimental investigations into clinical paradigms. In order to make quick advancement, more than double genome-wide association study of antimicrobial or antidepressant therapies must be underway as early as possible. Next generation sequencing (NGS) techniques will increase the speed of genome sequencing (15,000-50,000 times) and dramatically reduce the cost of genome sequencing (less than ten thousand US dollar for one genome) [Collins, 2010, Lander, 2011, Venter, 2011]. In future, genome sequencing working forces and researchers may be changed from biomedical major students into mathematic or physics major students or scholars [Lu et al., 2014]. Only enough genetic information of neural response or risk for antimicrobials has been obtained and accumulated, antimicrobials can be used safe and effective in future. After large scale and sized genetic or bioinformatics study, antimicrobials treatments will be pre-warned for all potential affected patients in future [Lu et al., 2012b, Lu et al., 2014].

DISCUSSION AND FUTURE TRENDS

In the future, we can pinpoint more genetic polymorphisms and toxicological mechanisms of action in order to explain drug-induced neural toxicity from different angles (mania, suicide and oto-toxicity [Li et al., 2005, Lu et al., 2010, Scrimshaw et al., 1999, Xie et al., 1997, Xing et al., 2006] and by different types of drugs—including antimicrobials and antidepressants [Lu et al., 2013, Lu et al., 2014]. It is an important area for us to focus and shed new light into modern neural science researches and drug development paradigms.

Roadmap and Possible Avenues for Further Investigations

Integration of drug toxic (madness and suicidal ideations)—disease progression (patients' depression)-score index into one system and make them available for experimental or clinical therapeutic studies and applications.

Support and promote novel ideas and techniques that help and fuel the assessments of new generation of hypotheses.

Create and finding more effective patents that help implementing antidepressant or antimicrobials treatment and risk/response evaluating and prediction systems in future [Lu et al., 2014].

Investigations of neural related genes, biological molecules and their pathogenic functions by new generations of technologies such as opto-genetics study [Lu et al., 2013, Zhao et al., 2013] or genetic engineering mice (GEM) [Youngtrom & Strowbridge, 2012] and so on.

Systems biology, mathematics and calculating models/systems investigations for in-depth understanding the intrinsic relationship between diagnosis and therapeutics.

Drafting more human genomes (large sizes of individuals and populations) and finding the relationship between different genetics or bioinformatics and risk/response by different types of antimicrobials.

Scientifically investigating on the relationship between pathogenesis and therapeutics of antidepressants and antimicrobials treatments from drug metabolisms and plasma concentrations [Kuo et al., 2013].

Collect data of relationship between genetics, molecular, chemical and environmental factors and drug (antimicrobials) efficacies and neural toxicities.

Genome-wide association study (GWAS) of more depressed patients and normal persons of different pathogenic conditions, ethnic groups/races, family inheritable diseases, genders or ages. For these work, worldwide cooperation and scientific investigations among different disciplinary scientists are urgently needed.

Genetic or genomic study of repeated DNA in human genomes and make a difference in new drug discoveries and development from these efforts and ideas [Lu et al., 2013, Lu et al., 2014].

Invitation of more mathematics or physics major students and scholars to join hands with biomedical major students and scientists in genomic sequencing, data analysis and clinical therapeutic efficacies and toxicities predictions [Lu et al., 2014].

Accumulating rare family inherence disease cases of human genomes as many as possible and GWAS study of inherent diseases are welcomed.

Budget control of all these scientific investigations and clinical antimicrobials treatment patients and affected individuals.

CONCLUSION

Suicide is a serious adverse toxicity for clinical drug utilizations—including antimicrobials applications. The systematic investigations and discovery of their mechanisms of action by antimicrobial interventions are indispensable parts of neural pathogenesis and toxicological sciences. These researches, as we guess, can make a difference in drug discovery, developments and licensing new generations of antimicrobials world-wide and safe clinical antimicrobial applications.

REFERENCES

Abouesh, A, et al. (2002). Antimicrobial-induced mania (antibiomania): a review of spontaneous reports. *J Clin Psychopharmacol. 22*, 71-81.

Baranowski, W. J. (2010). Clarithromycin-induced hypomania in a child—a case report. *Acta Psychiatr Scand*, *122*, 267-268.

Brent D., et al. (2010). Pharmacogenomics of suicidal events. *Pharmacogenomics. 11*(6), 793-807.

Check, E. (2004). Drug suicide risks prompt call for FDA action. *Nature*, *427*(6974), 474.

Collins, F. (2010). Has the revolution arrived. *Nature*, 464 (7289), 674-675.

Duffy, D. (2009). Self-injury. *Psychiatry*, *8*(7), 237-240.

Fidan, T. & Fidan, V. (2009). Clarithromycin-induced mania in a child. *Int J Clinical Pharmacol Therapeutics*, *47* (6), 402-404.

Garriock, H. A., et al. (2010). A genome wide association study of citalopram response in major depressive disorder. *Biol Psychiatry*, *67* (2), 133-138.

Holden, C. (2004). FDA weighs suicide risk in children on antidepressants. *Science (Washington DC)*, *303* (5659), 745.

Ingelman-Sundberg, M. (2005). Genetic polymorphisms of cytochrome P450 2D6 (CYP2D6): clinical consequences, evolutionary aspects and functional diversity. *Pharmacogenomics J.*, 5, 6-13.

Kapur, N. & Gask, L. (2009). Introduction to suicide and self-harm. *Psychiatry*, 2009, *8*(7), 233-236.

Kuo, H. W., et al. (2013). CYP1A2 genetic polymorphisms are associated with early antidepressant escitalopram metabolism and adverse reactions. *Pharmacogenomics*, *14*(10), 1191-1201.

Laje, G., et al. (2009). Genome-wide association study of suicidal ideation emerging during citalopram treatment of depressed outpatients. *Pharmacogenet Genomics*, *19* (9), 666-674.

Lander, E. S. (2011). Initial impact of the sequencing of the human genome. *Nature*, *470* (7333), 187-197.

Li, Z. Y. et al. (2005). Mutational analysis of the mitochondrial 12S rRNA gene in Chinese pediatric subjects with aminoglycoside-induced and non-syndromic hearing loss. *Human Genet*, *117* (1), 9-15.

Lu, D. Y., et al. (2007). May genetic factors play a role in the risk of antidepressant-induced suicide. *Med Hypotheses*. *69*, 1380-1381.

Lu, D. Y., et al. (2010). Undesired neural side-effects of a drug, a chemical and genetic interrelated problem. *Central Nervous System Agents in Medicinal Chemistry*. *10*(2), 108-112.

Lu, D. Y., et al. (2012a). The hypotheses for the pathogeny of drug-induced mania and suicide. *Cell Dev Biol*, *1* (4). e111.

Lu, D. Y., et al. (2012b). Genetics in neural toxicities of drugs. *Central Nervous System Agent Medicinal Chemistry*, *12* (4), 250-253.

Lu, D. Y., et al. (2013). Pharmacogenetics in neural toxicities of drugs. *Pharmacogenomics*, *14* (10), 1129-1131.

Lu, D. Y., et al. (2014). Genetics and bioinformatics studies of antidepressant drug therapeutic efficacies and toxicities, a current overview. *Recent Pat CNS Drug Discov*, *9*(3), 193-199.

Menke, A., et al. (2012). Genome-wide association study of antidepressant treatment-emergent suicidal ideation. *Neuropsychopharmacology*, *37*(3), 797-807.

Menke, A., et al. (2012). Polymorphisms within the metabotropic glutamate receptor 1 gene are associated with depression phenotypes. *Psychneuroendocrinology*, *37*(4), 565-575.

Scrimshaw, B. J., et al. (1999). Rapid identification of an A1555G mutation in human mitochondrial DNA implicated in aminoglycoside-induced ototoxicity. *J Human Genet*, 44 (5), 388-390.

Shah, R. R. (2006). Can pharmacogenetics help rescue drugs withdrawn from the market? *Pharmacogenomics*, *7*(6), 889-908.

Taylor, S. & Stein, M. B. (2006). The future of selective serotonin reuptake inhibitors (SSRIs). in psychiatric treatment. *Med Hypotheses.*, *66*, 14-21.

Tome, A. M. & Filipe, A. (2011). Quinolones: review of psychiatric and neurological adverse reaction. *Drug Safety*, *34*(6), 465-488.

Uher, R., et al. (2010). Genome-wide pharmacogenetics of antidepressant response in the GENDEP project. Am J *Psychiatry*, *167* (5), 555-564.

Venter, J. C. (2010). Multiple personal genomes await. *Nature*, *464* (7289), 676-677.

Xie, A. P. et al. (1997). Mutation in the mitochondrial 12S rRNA gene in two families from Mongolia with matrilineal aminoglycoside ototoxicity. *J Med Genet*, *34* (2), 169-172.

Xing, G. Q. et al. (2006). Mitochobdrial 12S rRNA A827G mutation is involved in the genetic susceptibility to aminoglycoside ototoxicity. *BBRC*, *346* (4), 1131-1135.

Youngtrom, I. A. & Strowbridge, B. W. (2012). Visual landmarks facilitate rodent, spatial navigation in virtual reality environment. *Learn Mem*, *9* (3), 84-90.

Zhao, Y. et al. (2013). Human dopamine transporter gene: differential regulation of 18-kb haplotypes. *Pharmacogenomics*, *14*(12), 1481-1494.

In: Suicidal Ideation
Editor: Bradley Weaver

ISBN: 978-1-63483-092-8

Chapter 5

SUICIDE PREVENTION USING THE INTERNET: MINI-REVIEW AND A CASE STUDY IN ONLINE GATEKEEPING ACTIVITY

Hajime Sueki*
Department of Psychology and Education, Faculty of Human Sciences, Wako University, Tokyo, Japan

ABSTRACT

In communities including many people with high suicide risk, nurturing gatekeepers are effective in preventing suicide. Evidence regarding suicide prevention through gatekeeping has been obtained at a quasi-experimental level. In recent years, novel attempts have been made to provide a basis for gatekeeping, such as extracting internet data indicating a high risk of suicide. Associations between suicide rates and web searches or Twitter use including suicide-related keywords have been reported in a large number of studies. These studies suggest the possibility of guiding people with high risk of suicide toward help resources by placing advertisements on the web. In Japan, a private non-profit organization called OVA has been engaged in online gatekeeping since 2013, by using search advertising techniques for those at high risk of suicide.

---

* Corresponding author: Hajime Sueki: Department of Psychology and Education, Faculty of Human Sciences, Wako University, 2160 Kanaimachi, Machida, Tokyo, 195-8585, Japan. E-mail: h_sueki@wako.ac.jp, Phone: +81-44-989-7777 (Ext.5911).

This chapter describes the online gatekeeping practice and discusses the feasibility and effects of online gatekeeping. Given the growing rate of Internet use worldwide, we should consider the effective utilization of this technology in order to prevent suicide.

INTRODUCTION

When thinking about suicide prevention in the modern age, it is extremely important to consider the influence and role of new media such as the Internet. Internet use is on the rise throughout the world, and its importance will likely continue to increase in the future. In Japan, use of the Internet in suicide prevention is included in the government's compiled policy, "Outline of Comprehensive Measures for Suicide Prevention". Specifically, this policy includes the need to use the Internet actively to promote the dissemination of correct information and to restrict information about suicide methods on the Internet (Japanese Cabinet Office, 2012).

Thus far, the Internet has been considered a problematic, harmful form of media in the realm of suicide prevention, and there has been much debate concerning how to minimize its influence. This is because the Internet has been a source of information about effective suicide methods. In approximately the year 2000, the phenomenon of so-called "Internet suicide pacts" arose in Japan (Naito, 2007; Ozawa-de Silva, 2008). This phenomenon is when multiple people who meet on anonymous electronic bulletin/ messaging boards commit group suicide. The main method of death for these members of suicide pacts has been carbon monoxide poisoning using briquettes. Group suicide participants are recruited over the Internet, and information regarding suicide methods is spread via the Internet. Additionally, since 2007, descriptions of suicide methods using hydrogen sulfide have been circulating around the Web (Morii, Miyagatani, Nakamae, Murao, and Taniyama, 2010), and cluster suicides increased when incidents of suicides employing this method were reported on television. Prior to 2008, there were almost no suicides by hydrogen sulfide. In 2008, however, over 1,000 people died by this method (Japanese Cabinet Office, 2010). A number of studies have acknowledged the media's influence in this matter and report that media coverage of suicide leads to further suicides (Stack, 2003).

However, the media does not always foster or encourage suicide. While some suicide coverage and dissemination of suicide information may trigger suicides, depending on the type of news coverage, suicide coverage can also prevent suicide. For example, if along with the suicide coverage, contact information for obtaining help were provided to people who saw the news and were in danger of committing suicide themselves, this type of coverage would be more likely to function as suicide prevention (Jobes, Berman, O'Carroll, Eastgard, and Knickmeyer, 1996). The media itself is not bad, but as a tool, depending on how it is used, media can work in both positive and negative ways.

The most well-known method that uses media for suicide prevention, and that is still being implemented, is telephone crisis intervention. In Japan, volunteers provide telephone counseling to people at high risk for suicide. These types of programs commonly operate in countries that have developed some level of infrastructure. There is insufficient evidence regarding the effectiveness of telephone crisis intervention programs in suicide prevention (World Health Organization, 2014). However, the World Health Organization (2014) indicates that this type of intervention has proved to be a useful and widely implemented best practice.

SUICIDE PREVENTION USING THE INTERNET

How can the Internet be used for suicide prevention? Internet suicide prevention can be divided into three main activities: promoting specialist interventions, providing peer support, and matching help resources.

Promotion of Specialist Interventions

Many specialist services, and much information about them, have become available online. Information related to suicide prevention can be divided into three types: E-therapy, which provides a type of psychotherapy over the Internet; education services related to suicide prevention that target mainly specialists and support providers; and websites geared toward the general public. A certain amount of evidence regarding the effectiveness of E-therapy (Christensen et al., 2013; van Spijker, Majo, Smit, van Straten, and Kerkhof, 2012; van Spijker, van Straten, and Kerkhof, 2014; Watts, Newby, Mewton, and Andrews, 2012) and suicide prevention education has been gathered. E-therapy has been shown to directly reduce suicidal ideation and treat depression, which is usually the underlying emotion behind suicide. Although suicide prevention education does not contribute directly to prevention, it can be expected to have an indirect effect, such as contributing to suicide prevention by way of gatekeeping and providing training support.

E-therapy is considered to have some effect on suicide prevention. One type, Internet Cognitive Behavioral Therapy (iCBT), reduces suicidal ideation. Many studies have reported iCBT's effectiveness (Christensen et al., 2013; van Spijkeret al., 2012; van Spijker at al., 2014; Watts et al., 2012). Of these, there has only been one randomized controlled study of iCBT that specialized in suicide prevention (van Spijker et al., 2014), and this study showed a reduction of suicidal ideation following iCBT. However, the effect sizes were all small. Furthermore, the fact that these studies' dependent variables were not completed suicides or suicide attempts is a limiting point. Compared with other measures, however, the quality of the research design and the evidence obtained was high. In addition, an even stronger effect was seen between iCBT and depression, a suicide risk factor. The UK's National Institute for Clinical Excellence (NICE, 2009) includes iCBT in its guidelines for depression treatment. It is possible that iCBT for depression may contribute to suicide prevention by providing low-cost psychotherapy with proven effectiveness.

One effective suicide prevention strategy is to quickly identify high-risk individuals within communities that have a large number of people at high risk for suicide and train gatekeepers who can connect these high-risk individuals with aid resources (Mannet al., 2005). Gatekeeper training is an established method with proven effectiveness (Isaac et al., 2009). Generally, when people participate in these types of programs, knowledge of suicide and suicide prevention increases, along with a sense of self-efficacy regarding crisis intervention. Some gatekeeper education programs have already gone online and have been proven to be effective (Lancaster et al., 2014).

By making online gatekeeper training/education programs available among Web communities with large numbers of people at high risk for suicide, we can expect to generate favorable suicide prevention results.

The operational status and effects of suicide prevention websites created for the general public have also been partially verified. The websites introduced here differ from the aforementioned E-therapy and suicide prevention education websites in that they are not created with a limited purpose (for example, treatment or education). A questionnaire for viewers of suicide prevention websites (Sueki, 2010) suggests that quite a few of these viewers happen upon these websites while searching for Internet suicide partners and effective suicide methods. In addition, it indicates that obtaining objective information about suicide can possibly reduce suicidal ideation by promoting an understanding of suicide.

Limiting cognitive and physical access to suicide methods leads to suicide prevention (Florentine and Crane, 2010). Although there are a number of methods for reducing access to information about suicide methods on the Internet, it is difficult to get the moderators of suicide-related websites to change their content (Jorm, Fischer, and Oh, 2010). In addition, there are limits to regulating websites that contain information on suicide methods; therefore, it is important to increase the number of websites that contain new information on suicide prevention.

Providing Peer Support

Peer support occupies an extremely important position within suicide prevention methods because it can potentially reduce loneliness, a factor that increases suicide risk (van Orden et al., 2010). Telephone crisis intervention is an example of a media-friendly peer-support suicide prevention activity. As the Internet spread, a new type of peer support arose—the direct exchange of messages among people at high risk for suicide. Unfortunately, it is difficult to say that the effects of this type of activity contribute to suicide prevention.

An example of research related to peer support on the Internet is the literature on the activities that take place on suicide websites and their effects. While people transmit information on effective suicide methods using electronic bulletin boards on these websites, mental health guidance simultaneously occurs on these sites among people with heightened suicide risk (Sueki and Eichenberg, 2012). Although suicide websites have gained attention as contributing to Internet suicides, a problem growing since the early 2000s, they possess two contradictory functions. They are not only a place for transmitting suicide methods, but also, they are a place for offering peer support. Many specialists note this paradoxical functionality of suicide sites (Biddle, Donovan, Hawton, Kapur, and Gunnell, 2008; Luxton, June, and Fairall, 2012; Sisask and Värnik, 2012).

The most reliable study to investigate the impact of suicide-site use suggests that use does not have preventative effects, but rather, suicide-inducing effects (Sueki, Yonemoto, Takeshima, and Inagaki, 2014). More specifically, the study shows that confessing feelings of wanting to die to anonymous others and viewing suicide methods are associated with suicide ideation aggravation, and consulting with anonymous others about mental health is associated with the aggravation of depression and anxiety. In most cases, confiding in and consulting with anonymous others who can be easily contacted on the Internet does not alleviate suicidal ideation; conversely, it strengthens those feelings. To date, there have been no rigorous studies investigating why this happens. One contributing factor is thought to be the fact that when consultation occurs among anonymous, non-specialists over the Internet, an appropriate response to those with imminent suicide danger is not always available.

Crisis intervention and consultation activities using trained volunteers through e-mail, online chats, and online bulletin boards have been increasing throughout the world (Barak, 2007; Gilat and Shahar, 2009). Although no research has yet studied the effects of these activities quantitatively, one study did investigate them qualitatively (Greidanus and Everall, 2010). In this study, a consultation location was created using an online bulletin board, and trained volunteers monitored the board 24 hours a day. When mutual consultation activities were encouraged, more empathetic comments and advice were seen among the exchanges, and it was concluded that a helper therapy effect occurred. The alleviation of loneliness through peer support is an important suicide prevention activity; however, when peer support takes place over the Internet and is not appropriately moderated, it is possible that the support will have a suicide-inducing effect. While implementing these types of activities, it is necessary to have the participation of volunteers with solid specialized knowledge and some level of training.

Help-Resource Matching

The matching of help resources is the act of bridging the gap between the potential help needs of people dealing with various problems and setting up an environment in which to deliver the necessary support to those in need. People needing help—i.e., people at high risk for suicide—vacillate between wanting to die and wanting to live (Shneidman, 1993). For this reason, it is difficult for them to seek help voluntarily. However, their feelings of wanting to live are often stronger than their feelings of wanting to die. Therefore, it is desirable to use the Internet to prepare an environment in which high-risk individuals can appropriately take advantage of specialized support to live better.

Representative studies on support resource matching via the Internet found people at high risk for suicide by using search engine data (Gunn and Lester, 2013; Hagihara, Miyazaki, and Abe, 2012; McCarthy, 2010; Sueki, 2011; Yang, Tsai, Huang, and Peng, 2011). It is anticipated that with these types of studies, if people at high risk for suicide enter suicide-related search words into Web searches, such as "I want to die," "I want to commit suicide," or "suicide methods," this will result in advertisements being shown that are related to the search and may potentially connect them to support resources. These studies that discover the existence of, and spread information on, all kinds of problems, including suicide, through search-engine histories fit into the field of infodemiology.

Through these studies, a connection has been discovered between suicide and searches for suicide-related words. The most common type of study investigates the time-series and regional relationships between the volume of suicide-related word searches and suicide rates (Gunn and Lester, 2013; Hagihara at al., 2012; McCarthy, 2010; Sueki, 2011; Yang et al., 2011). The rate of enacting suicide-related behaviors is significantly higher among people who searched for suicide-related words compared with those who had not (Sueki, 2012). Additionally, some reports confirm that among several completed suicides, Internet searches for suicide methods were performed immediately before the suicide occurred (Gunnell et al., 2012). As the aforementioned research shows, there is a clear relationship between Web-based searches for suicide-related words and suicide occurrence.

Because people performing Internet searches for suicide-related words are at high risk for committing suicide, by serving such users suicide-prevention advertisements in response to their searches, it is more likely that the searchers will access the necessary help resources. For example, since the 2000s, there has been an attempt to display results including a help-resources website with contact information whenever suicide-related words are entered into Yahoo! JAPAN's search engine. Additional examples of efforts to connect people at high risk for suicide with appropriate help resources via advertisements in suicide-related Web searches include applications such as Gatekeeper 2.0 (Sueki, 2013). Gatekeeper 2.0 is part of the attempt to display advertisements in response to Web searches with the intent to solicit e-mail consultations and connect individuals with personal help resources (e.g., psychiatric consultation). The 2013 Gatekeeper 2.0 activity records (Sueki, 2013) showed that the average age of the consulters was 23.8 (standard deviation = 9.7). Approximately 80% were female, and suicidal ideation was seen in about 70% of the consulters. A positive mood change (including postponement of a suicide attempt) was seen in 10.8% of the individuals as a result of e-mail consultation, and about 10.1% of the people actually began to seek help. Therefore, with the Gatekeeper 2.0 program, it may be possible to collect consultation e-mails from young people and spur suicide-preventing changes among certain users.

GATEKEEPER 2.0

The aforementioned practices that use the research results of help-resource matching are promising for suicide prevention. This is because training gatekeepers in communities that have many people at high risk for suicide is an effective suicide prevention strategy (Knox, Litts, Talcott, Feig, and Caine, 2003; Rutz, Knorring, and Wålinder, 1992). Therefore, although the effectiveness of using Internet-behavior history to quickly identify people at high risk for suicide and connect them to appropriate help resources has not yet been verified, it is highly possible that the Gatekeeper 2.0 will be effective in preventing suicide. Below, I report on the actual activities of Gatekeeper 2.0 as implemented by the non-profit organization OVA. After introducing the detailed state of progress of help cases, the factors that allowed the online gatekeeper's activities to succeed will be discussed. In the case descriptions, the total number of e-mail consultation exchanges is noted with "#," and the consultation day is marked by "X". Although some content from these cases has been modified to protect privacy, these case reports are basically created from the actual records of e-mail consultations. The consulters provided informed consent to use their consultation records for research.

Case 1: Man *A* (53 Years Old)

Man *A* saw the advertisement for Gatekeeper 2.0 when he searched for the words "I want to die", which resulted in his sending a consultation e-mail. In the first e-mail (#1), Man *A* wrote a polite self-introduction and detailed his present troubles. Some years ago, he left his office as a result of interpersonal relationship troubles with his boss. Since then, he has been shut away in his house, living off savings. Presently, although he still possesses some cash, his debt has ballooned. He became estranged from his parents and siblings when he was younger and was not in a position to receive assistance from them. His e-mail indicated that he had fairly high levels of anxiety and irritability from financial troubles that would arise in the future. The results from an online questionnaire sent for assessment purposes (#2) showed that he earned 30 points (out of 30) on the Japanese version of the K6 (Kessler et al., 2002; Furukawa et al., 2008), which is a screening tool for depression and anxiety disorders. In addition, he had a history of suicidal ideation and plans for suicide, as well as multiple suicide attempts.

It was also revealed that he drank alcohol almost every day. Presently, however, he did not have any specific plans for suicide.

#3 – 30 (~ X + Day 7) The gatekeeper suggested that while he still had cash, the consulter needed to reorganize his life. To do this, he should first check in at a psychiatric hospital to improve his mental health. Man *A* agreed with the recommendation; however, he reported an experience he had had several years ago when he received hurtful remarks from a psychiatrist he had visited for insomnia troubles. For Man *A*, it was difficult to take action toward making an office visit because he feared the doctor would not understand him. After hearing about his past visits, the gatekeeper guessed it was Man *A*'s strong belief that he should "remain strong" and "stand firm" in the examination room that caused poor communication with the doctor. The gatekeeper conducted an Internet search with him for a hospital that would be easy to travel to from Man *A*'s residence. After contacting the hospital's office, the gatekeeper informed Man *A* of how to make an appointment. Although Man *A* repeatedly delayed the scheduling of the office visit, he finally called to make an appointment.

#31 – 40 (~ X + Day 10) Man *A* reported by e-mail that he had visited the hospital, was told by the doctor he might have bipolar disorder, and was prescribed medication. Man *A* happily shared that he believed the attending physician and felt positive about wanting treatment. He also reported that he was now able to attend religious services, which he had been unable to attend for some time. The consultation concluded with an understanding that it was acceptable to e-mail anytime he had any issue.

Case 2: Woman *B* (22 Years Old)

Woman *B* searched for suicide methods after she learned she would repeat a year of school at the university. At approximately the same time, her boyfriend of four years, to whom she had been engaged, broke off the engagement. When she searched for the words "ways to die," the Gatekeeper 2.0 advertisement caught her eye, and she sent a consultation e-mail. Her first e-mail was similar to a suicide note of about 700 characters. Her family's finances were tight, and she couldn't bear to burden her family financially any further. Additionally, the fiancé she loved had dumped her, and it seemed she had not been able to eat properly for a week. As a specific suicide method, she mentioned she wanted to continue like this and starve to death. The results of the online questionnaire that was sent for assessment purposes showed she earned 22 (out of 30) points on the K6. Although she had suicidal ideation and plans for suicide, she had no history of suicide attempts. She had no friends she could rely on at the university. Her ex-fiancé was the only person with whom she felt comfortable. Worried about Woman *B*'s situation and her living alone, the gatekeeper hurriedly proposed to communicate over the phone, and Woman *B* agreed. There was no strength in her voice, and she could barely be heard over the phone. Upon insistence from Woman *B* that e-mail exchanges were preferable to speaking, they decided to continue communicating via e-mail from that point on.

#3–10 (~X + Day 4) Considering the woman's health issues, the gatekeeper suggested the woman's parents come to her residence, but Woman *B* adamantly refused. To Woman *B*, not being able to meet the expectations of her parents, who, despite the family's tight finances, had allowed her to live on her own and had created an environment for her to commit to her studies, was the most unbearable thing of all. It seemed that having to repeat a year at school had brought on an incredible sense of loss for Woman *B*, who had been committed to her studies since elementary school and prided herself on being good at studying.

#11 – 17 (~ X + Day 7) While talking about her feelings toward her parents through e-mail, Woman *B* decided she should return home and tell her parents about having to repeat a year at school. However, because she thought repeating a year would disappoint her parents and next year's tuition and living expenses would bring further financial burden, she could not bring herself to do it. The gatekeeper continued replying to her e-mails in an attempt to clarify Woman *B*'s ambivalent feelings.

#18 – 21 (~ X + Day 21) Two weeks later, Woman *B* reported that she had returned home and had been able to tell her parents about the need to repeat a year. Additionally, she would spend time recuperating at home.

Ways to Encourage Help-Seeking Behavior

With Gatekeeper 2.0, consulters are not only being connected to psychiatric consultations, but also to the help resources deemed necessary by the gatekeeper upon assessment of the consulter's situation.

While psychiatric consultations are commonly recommended via e-mail consultations, few people immediately visit a psychiatrist's office after receiving the recommendation.

Also, many consulters are hesitant to confide in people close to them about their troubles. Many people experience a reduced desire to seek help when they are in a high suicide-risk state.

Based on the above cases, several actions were found to encourage consultation and help-seeking behaviors in people at high risk for suicide: 1) working hard to expand/amplify the contradictions within the consulter, 2) repeating the words related to help-seeking used by the consulter as a way of empathizing, and 3) acting with them specifically to reduce help-seeking costs.

Generally, consulters are in an ambivalent state, vacillating between feelings of wanting to die and wanting to live. Additionally, in most cases, the consulters express in their e-mails that they feel something catastrophic has happened to them, and that it might be better to receive help from someone. As shown in Case 2, by clarifying the consulter's ambivalent thoughts, it was possible to transform the consulter's attitude toward seeking help.

Furthermore, it is extremely important to reduce help-seeking costs for the consulter, and the gatekeeper must work with the consulter to accomplish this. In Case 1, the gatekeeper searched for a hospital along with the consulter, while also performing interventions to reduce the anxiety the consulter felt toward the future psychiatric consultation. These points are consistent with the theory of motivational interviewing (Britton, Williams, and Conner, 2008; Britton, Conner, and Maisto, 2012).

However, there remain plenty of difficulties with these activities. Although both cases presented in this paper were cases in which the support worked well, only 10% of the confirmed cases led to new face-to-face help resources with the aid of the online gatekeepers' activities.

That is, these techniques alone are inadequate as suicide prevention support. To increase this percentage, it is necessary to gather research on support model and communication techniques.

CONCLUSION

It is believed that, in the future, there will be more attempts at early identification and intervention for people grappling with specific problems via the analysis of lifelogs left inadvertently on the Web by Internet users, such as those obtained through search engine histories. Currently, although directing advertisements during Web searches at high-risk individuals is the most efficient way of discovering and supporting them, the methods used in this trend will likely change along with technological development.

It may also be possible to improve screening accuracy by using additional information from social networking services (Sueki, 2015).

In either case, it will be important to maintain tireless efforts to continue appropriately reforming models using current technology. When using Web lifelogs to quickly discover people at high risk for suicide and connect them with the appropriate help destinations, it is necessary to refine and systematize techniques for connecting those who are deliberating about whether they need to seek help, with places of support. Although there has been a wealth of research on motivation within the field of psychology, the current findings must be considered (Britton, Williams, and Conner, 2008; Britton, Conner, and Maisto, 2012), along with the psychological conditions of those at high risk for suicide, as new communication technologies continue to be applied to suicide prevention.

It is both possible and important to study the effects of new services available on the Internet; however, the speed of research cannot maintain pace with the speed at which new services and technologies are introduced. Therefore, by the time studies examining the effects of certain services and technologies are completed, no one is using those services and technologies any longer. This phenomenon easily occurs in fields that study support obtained via the Internet. It is therefore necessary to study not only the influences of specific services and technologies, but additional points, such as what types of people are susceptible to negative influences from new services and technologies, and what can be done to keep those people from becoming at high risk for committing suicide.

New communication technologies and services are created with the intent to improve our lives; however, sometimes they also lead to negative effects. If we can study which people have characteristics that make them susceptible to experiencing these negative effects, we may be able to use this information to formulate suicide prevention measures quickly when developing technologies and services for future generations.

REFERENCES

Barak, A. (2007). Emotional support and suicide prevention through the Internet: A field project study. *Computers in Human Behavior*, 23, 971-984.

Biddle, L., Donovan, J., Hawton, K., Kapur, N., and Gunnell, D. (2008). Suicide and the internet. *British Medical Journal*, 336, 800-802.

Britton, P. C., Williams, G. C. and Conner, K. R. (2008). Self-determination theory, motivational interviewing, and the treatment of clients with acute suicidal ideation. *Journal of Clinical Psychology*, 64, 52-66.

Britton, P. C., Conner, K. R. and Maisto, S. A. (2012). An open trial of motivational interviewing to address suicidal ideation with hospitalized veterans. *Journal of Clinical Psychology*, 68, 961-971.

Christensen, H., Farrer, L., Batterham, P. J., Mackinnon, A., Griffiths, K. M., and Donker, T. (2013). The effect of a web-based depression intervention on suicide ideation: secondary outcome from a randomised controlled trial in a helpline. *BMJ open*, 3, e002886.

Florentine, J. B. and Crane, C. (2010). Suicide prevention by limiting access to methods: a review of theory and practice. *Social Science and Medicine*, 70, 1626-1632.

Furukawa, T. A., Kawakami, N., Saitoh, M., Ono, Y., Nakane, Y., Nakamura, Y., ... and Kikkawa, T. (2008). The performance of the Japanese version of the K6 and K10 in the World Mental Health Survey Japan. *International Journal of Methods in Psychiatric Research*, 17, 152-158.

Gilat, I. and Shahar, G. (2009). Suicide prevention by online support groups: An action theory-based model of emotional first aid. *Archives of Suicide Research*, 13, 52-63.

Greidanus, E. and Everall, R. D. (2010). Helper therapy in an online suicide prevention community. *British Journal of Guidance and Counselling*, 38, 191-204.

Gunn III, J. F. and Lester, D. (2013). Using google searches on the internet to monitor suicidal behavior. *Journal of Affective Disorders*, 148, 411-412.

Gunnell, D., Bennewith, O., Kapur, N., Simkin, S., Cooper, J., and Hawton, K. (2012). The use of the Internet by people who die by suicide in England: A cross sectional study. *Journal of Affective Disorders*, 141, 480-483.

Hagihara, A., Miyazaki, S. and Abe, T. (2012). Internet suicide searches and the incidence of suicide in young people in Japan. *European Archives of Psychiatry and Clinical Neuroscience*, 262, 39-46.

Isaac, M., Elias, B., Katz, L. Y., Belik, S. L., Deane, F. P., Enns, M. W., andSareen, J. (2009). Gatekeeper training as a preventative intervention for suicide: a systematic review. *Canadian Journal of Psychiatry*, 54, 260-268.

Japanese Cabinet Office, Government of Japan (2012). Outline of comprehensive measures for suicide prevention. Available: http://www8.cao.go.jp/jisatsutaisaku/taikou/index_20120828.html Accessed 2014 June 18.

Japanese Cabinet Office, Government of Japan (2010). *2009 White paper on suicide prevention in Japan.* Available: http://www8.cao.go.jp/jisatsutaisaku/whitepaper/index-w.htmlAccessed 2014 June 18.

Jobes, D. A., Berman, A. L., O'Carroll, P. W., Eastgard, S., and Knickmeyer, S. (1996). The Kurt Cobain suicide crisis: Perspectives from research, public health, and the news media. *Suicide and Life-Threatening Behavior*, 26, 260-271.

Jorm, A. F., Fischer, J. A. and Oh, E. (2010). Effect of feedback on the quality of suicide prevention websites: randomised controlled trial. *British Journal of Psychiatry*, 197, 73-74.

Kessler, R. C., Andrews, G., Colpe, L. J., Hiripi, E., Mroczek, D. K., Normand, S. L., ... and Zaslavsky, A. M. (2002). Short screening scales to monitor population prevalences and trends in non-specific psychological distress. *Psychological Medicine*, 32, 959-976.

Knox, K. L., Litts, D. A., Talcott, G. W., Feig, J. C., and Caine, E. D. (2003). Risk of suicide and related adverse outcomes after exposure to a suicide prevention programme in the US Air Force: cohort study. *British Medical Journal*, 327, 1376.

Lancaster, P. G., Moore, J. T., Putter, S. E., Chen, P. Y., Cigularov, K. P., Baker, A., and Quinnett, P. (2014). Feasibility of a web-based gatekeeper training: Implications for suicide prevention. *Suicide and Life-Threatening Behavior*, 44, 510-523.

Luxton, D. D., June, J. D. and Fairall, J. M. (2012). Social media and suicide: A public health perspective. *American Journal of Public Health*, 102, S195-S200.

McCarthy, M. J. (2010). Internet monitoring of suicide risk in the population. *Journal of Affective Disorders*, 122, 277-279.

Mann, J. J., Apter, A., Bertolote, J., Beautrais, A., Currier, D., Haas, A., ... and Hendin, H. (2005). Suicide prevention strategies: a systematic review. *Journal of the American Medical Association*, 294, 2064-2074.

Morii, D., Miyagatani, Y., Nakamae, N., Murao, M., and Taniyama, K. (2010). Japanese experience of hydrogen sulfide: the suicide craze in 2008. *Journal of Occupational Medicine and Toxicology*, 5, 28-28.

Naito, A. (2007). Internet suicide in Japan: implications for child and adolescent mental health. *Clinical Child Psychology and Psychiatry*, 12, 583-597.

National Institute for Clinical Excellence (2009). Depression in adults: The treatment and management of depression in adults. Available: https://www.nice.org.uk/guidance/cg90 Accessed 2014 October 31.

Ozawa-de Silva, C. (2008). Too lonely to die alone: Internet suicide pacts and existential suffering in Japan. *Culture, Medicine, and Psychiatry*, 32, 516-551.

Rutz, W., Knorring, L. V. and Wålinder, J. (1992). Long-term effects of an educational program for general practitioners given by the Swedish Committee for the Prevention and Treatment of Depression. *Acta Psychiatrica Scandinavica*, 85, 83-88.

Shneidman, E. S. (1993). *Suicide as psychache: A clinical approach to self-destructive behavior*. New York: Aronson.

Sisask, M. and Värnik, A. (2012). Media roles in suicide prevention: A systematic review. *International Journal of Environmental Research and Public Health*, 9, 123-138.

Stack, S. (2003). Media coverage as a risk factor in suicide. *Journal of Epidemiology and Community Health*, 57, 238-240.

Sueki, H. (2010). User characteristics of suicide-preventive information service on the internet and an effect of browsing he contents on users' suicidal ideation: comparison between minors and adults. *Suicide Prevention and Crisis Intervention*, 30, 23-30 (Japanese).

Sueki, H. (2011). Does the volume of Internet searches using suicide-related search terms influence the suicide death rate? : Data from 2004 to 2009 in Japan. *Psychiatry and Clinical Neurosciences*, 65, 392-394.

Sueki, H. (2012). Association between deliberate self-harm-related Internet searches and the mental states and lifetime suicidal behaviors of Japanese young adults. *Psychiatry and Clinical Neurosciences*, 66, 451-453.

Sueki, H. (2013). Internet gatekeeper/Night patrol 2.0. "Suicide prevention and collaboration with media." *The second meeting for the WHO World Suicide Report and Symposium* (December, 2013, Tokyo, Akihabara UDX).

Sueki, H. (2015). The association of suicide-related Twitter use with suicidal behaviour: A cross-sectional study of young internet users in Japan. *Journal of Affective Disorders*, 170, 155-160.

Sueki, H. and Eichenberg, C. (2012). Suicide bulletin board systems comparison between Japan and Germany. *Death Studies*, 36, 565-580.

Sueki, H., Yonemoto, N, Takeshima, T., and Inagaki, M. (2014). The impact of suicidality-related internet use: A prospective large cohort study with young and middle-aged internet users. *PloS ONE*, 9, e94841.

Van Orden, K. A., Witte, T. K., Cukrowicz, K. C., Braithwaite, S. R., Selby, E. A., and Joiner Jr, T. E. (2010). The interpersonal theory of suicide. *Psychological Review*, 117, 575-600.

Van Spijker, B. A., Majo, M. C., Smit, F., van Straten, A., and Kerkhof, A. J. (2012). Reducing suicidal ideation: cost-effectiveness analysis of a randomized controlled trial of unguided web-based self-help. *Journal of medical Internet research*, 14, e141.

Van Spijker, B. A., van Straten, A. and Kerkhof, A. J. (2014). Effectiveness of online self-help for suicidal thoughts: Results of a randomised controlled trial. *PloS one*, 9, e90118.

Watts, S., Newby, J. M., Mewton, L., and Andrews, G. (2012). A clinical audit of changes in suicide ideas with internet treatment for depression. *BMJ open*, 2, e001558.

World Health Organization (2014). *Preventing suicide: A global imperative.* Available: http://www.who.int/mental_health/suicide-prevention/world_report_2014/en/Accessed 2014 October 31.

Yang, A. C., Tsai, S. J., Huang, N. E., and Peng, C. K. (2011). Association of Internet search trends with suicide death in Taipei City, Taiwan, 2004–2009. *Journal of Affective Disorders*, 132, 179-184.

INDEX

A

G

H

I

J

K

L

M

Q

R

S

T

U

V

W

Y